A Feminist Guide to the Canadian Constitution

August 1992

Lynn Smith and Eleanor Wachtel

Canadian Advisory Council on the Status of Women

Prepared for the Canadian Advisory Council on the Status of Women
P.O. Box 1541, Station B
Ottawa, Ontario
K1P 5R5

This background paper was commissioned by the CACSW. Background papers are prepared to inform Council members, the general public, and parliamentarians on issues being considered by the CACSW. They are designed to provide an initial analysis on a subject and to generate public discussion.

The information contained in this background paper was provided by the authors, and does not necessarily reflect the views of the CACSW.

Available free of charge from the
Canadian Advisory Council on the Status of Women by quoting No. 92-L-186.
(The CACSW reserves the right to limit quantities)

Photocopying of CACSW Materials
Libraries may freely photocopy CACSW materials for traditional multiple library use, including multiple copies for reserve room use, extra copies for faculty/student dissemination, interlibrary loan, and network use. Our only stipulation is that the source be mentioned. The CACSW has no "per-charge" fee and does not participate in any individual royalty system.
Individual users may also reproduce material for classroom teaching and personal purposes, provided the source is mentioned.
Reproduction restriction of CACSW materials applies to the reprinting or anthologizing for commercial resale or publication; in which case permission should be obtained in writing from the Director of Communications, CACSW, P.O. Box 1541, Station B, Ottawa, Ontario K1P 5R5.

© Canadian Advisory Council on the Status of Women 1992

Canadian Cataloguing in Publication Data

Smith, Lynn, 1945 -

A Feminist guide to the Canadian constitution

Issued also in French under title: La Constitution canadienne : un guide féministe.
Includes bibliographical references.
ISBN 0-662-19785-2
DSS cat. no. LW31-36/1992E

1. Women -- Legal status, laws, etc. -- Canada.
2. Canada. Constitution Act, 1982. 3. Women's
rights -- Canada. 4. Sex discrimination
against women -- Law and legislation -- Canada.
Wachtel, Eleanor. II. Canadian Advisory Council
on the Status of Women. III. Title.

KE4381.S54 1992   342.71'0878   C92-099713-9

Dedication

This publication is dedicated to the memory of Renate Shearer, our beloved friend and a life-long advocate of human rights.

Acknowledgements

The authors wish to thank Megan Ellis, Maureen Roantree, Sarah Murphy, Cliona Kimber, and Catherine Dauvergne for their creative and diligent assistance in the research for this publication. They also thank Tina Head, of the Canadian Advisory Council on the Status of Women, for her thoughtful comments and encouragement, and Elly Silverman for her steadfast support of this project. The assistance of Robin Elliot in reading the manuscript at an early stage is also gratefully acknowledged.

Table of Contents

Preface vi

Chronology of Women and the Constitution vii

Introduction 1

What is a Constitution? 4

What is a Feminist Perspective? 8

What is the Canadian Constitution? 11

   Where is the Constitution Found? 11
   Formal Documents 11
   Conventions 12

   What are the Important Principles of Canada's Constitution? 15
   The Crown 15
   The Branches of Government 16
   Division of Powers 24
   Amending the Constitution 28
   Canadian Charter of Rights and Freedoms 29

How the Constitution Got This Way 44

   History Up to the Charter 44

   The Constitution Act, 1982 and its Aftermath 49

Conclusion 54

Notes 59

Bibliography 76

Preface

Canada's constitution is the subject of much longstanding debate across the country. The Canadian Advisory Council on the Status of Women (CACSW) has participated in that debate since its founding in 1973; it called for an equal rights amendment to the then *British North America Act*. Since that time, constitutional issues have been treated as part of the CACSW's mandate: to advise the federal government and inform the public on matters of concern to women.

Members of the CACSW meet with women in their communities and bring women's concerns to the attention of the full Council for discussion and action. CACSW members believe that women have both the right and the responsibility to actively participate in the political, economic, and social development of our country. To that end, Council members strongly believe that women's participation in constitutional debate and resolution is essential.

To help women respond to the challenge, the members identified a need within their communities for a guide to the development of Canada's constitution which would identify women's roles and interests in constitutional history. Three major questions needed to be addressed:

1) What is the Canadian constitution?
2) How and why has Canada's constitution evolved?
3) What does the constitution mean to women?

The CACSW commissioned this document to provide a framework within which the many constitutional issues can be analyzed from a feminist perspective. The authors were commissioned to review Canadian constitutional history up to the summer of 1990; thus, *A Feminist Guide to the Canadian Constitution* covers it only to that point. However, a few updates have been incorporated to reflect recent significant changes to the law.

The CACSW, and authors Lynn Smith and Eleanor Wachtel, firmly believe that Canada's constitution should be developed with the full participation of women so that it will work for women. All women in Canada are strongly urged to actively participate in debate on the constitution and in the implementation stages of any changes.

Chronology of Women and the Constitution

1763 The Treaty of Paris cedes New France to Great Britain.

The Royal Proclamation imposes English common law and criminal law systems on New France, provides for an elected assembly, and addresses some aspects of the relationship between European colonizers and Aboriginal peoples.

1763 – 1867 Treaties are signed with various First Nations; there is some participation of First Nations women as signatories to treaties.

1774 The *Quebec Act* restores the French civil law system to Quebec and provides for an appointed council (no provisions for an elected assembly).

All "persons" in Upper Canada who meet property requirement are enfranchised.

New Brunswick passes legislation specifically excluding women from voting.

1791 The *Constitutional Act* creates the provinces of Upper and Lower Canada, and provides for each to have an elected assembly.

1792 The first statute passed by the new legislature of Upper Canada makes English law applicable in the colony.

1809 – 1844 Some historical record of women voting.

1836 Prince Edward Island statute excludes women from voting.

1840 The *Union Act* joins Upper and Lower Canada in the united province of Canada, with a single legislature.

A Feminist Guide to the Canadian Constitution

1851 Nova Scotia passes law that specifically prohibits women from voting.

New Brunswick passes *An Act to Secure to Married Women Real and Personal Property Held in Their Own Right*, giving married women certain property rights.

1859 Ontario passes *An Act to Secure to Married Women Certain Separate Rights of Property*, removing some of the rights of husbands to control their wives' property.

1866 The Civil Code of Lower Canada comes into effect, restricting married women from entering into contracts or business or professions without their husbands' consent.

1867 The *British North America Act* (B.N.A. Act) provides for union of present-day Ontario, Quebec, Nova Scotia, and New Brunswick. The Act provides for division of powers between federal and provincial governments, and sets out basic structure of federal state. The Act remains the foundation of the Canadian Constitution.

1869 Aboriginal women who marry non-Aboriginal men lose rights accorded under the federal *Indian Act*.

1870 Manitoba enters Confederation.

1871 British Columbia enters Confederation.

1873 B.C. women who meet property and race requirements become first in Canada to get right to vote in municipal elections.

P.E.I. enters Confederation.

1874 Provisions of the *Indian Act* (see 1869 above) is extended uniformly across Canada.

1875 The Supreme Court of Canada is created by federal statute.

1885 The federal *Electoral Franchise Act* defines a "person" who may vote in federal elections as "a male person, including an Indian and excluding a person of Mongolian or Chinese origin".

1892 The right to vote in municipal and school matters is extended to "spinsters and widows" in Quebec.

1897 Clara Brett Martin is called to the Ontario Bar; she is the first woman in the British Empire to be called to the Bar.

1905 Supreme Court of New Brunswick refuses to allow a woman (Mabel Penery French) to practise law.

Alberta and Saskatchewan enter Confederation.

Chronology of Women and the Constitution

1906   New Brunswick passes legislation allowing women to practise law.

1916   Emily Murphy is appointed the first woman police magistrate in the Commonwealth (Edmonton).

1916 – 1919   Women in all provinces except P.E.I., Newfoundland, and Quebec win the right to vote in provincial elections (with restrictions remaining based on ancestry in some cases).

1917   Louise McKinney and Roberta MacAdams are elected in Alberta, the first women to be elected to any provincial legislature.

1918   Women who are not of Chinese, Japanese or East Indian ancestry, not "registered Indians" or Inuit, and not prisoners, "patients in lunatic asylums", or "receiving public charitable support", win the right to vote in federal elections.

Mary Ellen Smith is the first woman elected to the British Columbia legislature.

1919   M.O. Ramsland is the first woman elected to the Saskatchewan legislature.

1920   Women, not of the groups described above (see 1918), win the right to hold political office and sit in Parliament.

Edith Rogers is the first woman elected to the Manitoba legislature.

1921   Agnes Macphail becomes the first woman elected to the House of Commons.

Mary Ellen Smith (B.C.) becomes the first woman cabinet minister in the British Empire.

1922   P.E.I. women win the right to vote in provincial elections.

1925   Women over age 25 win the right to vote in provincial elections in Newfoundland.

1927   The *Indian Act* prohibits Aboriginal peoples from raising money or retaining lawyers to pursue land claims.

1928   The Supreme Court of Canada finds that women are not "qualified persons" and thus ineligible for appointment to the Senate.

1930   The British Privy Council reverses the Supreme Court of Canada and finds that women are eligible for appointment to the Senate.

Cairine Wilson (not one of the group that brought the case) becomes the first woman appointed to the Senate.

Lady Squires is the first woman elected to the Newfoundland legislature.

Chronology of Women and the Constitution

1931 The *Statute of Westminster* provides that the Parliament of Great Britain will not pass laws applicable to the Dominions, including Canada, except at the request and with the consent of the Dominion. The Statute also grants the Dominions the power to repeal or amend imperial statutes, except for the B.N.A. Act.

1934 Legislation barring women from holding seats in the New Brunswick legislature is repealed.

1940 Quebec women win the right to vote and to run for office in provincial elections.

1942 Internment of Japanese-Canadians begins.

1943 Agnes Macphail and Margarette "Rae" Morrison Luckock are the first women elected to the Ontario legislature.

Helen Kinnear is appointed County Court Judge in Ontario; she is the first woman in the British Empire to hold superior court judgeship.

1944 Disparities in provincial programs lead the federal government to take over family allowance program. Cheques are made payable to mothers.

Post World War II Years

The right to vote is extended (in various years) to Canadian women and men of Chinese, Japanese, and East Indian parentage.

Introduction of social welfare legislation (1951, *Old Age Security Act*; 1965, *Canada Pensions Act*; 1966, *Medical Care Insurance Act*).

1946 The *Canadian Citizenship Act* permits women marrying non-Canadians to retain Canadian citizenship.

The voting age for women in Newfoundland provincial elections is lowered to 21 (same as for men).

1949 Legislation abolishing appeals to the Judicial Committee of the Privy Council comes into force. The Supreme Court of Canada becomes Canada's court of final resort in all matters.

Newfoundland becomes Canada's tenth province.

1951 Ontario permits women to sit as jurors.

Manitoba women are permitted to sit as jurors. (Other provinces follow: New Brunswick in 1954, B.C. in 1964, P.E.I. in 1966, Quebec in 1976.)

Chronology of Women and the Constitution

1960　　The right to vote in federal elections is extended to status Indians.

　　　　　Gladys Porter is the first woman elected to the Nova Scotia legislature.

　　　　　The *Canadian Bill of Rights* is passed by the federal Parliament.

1962　　Claire Kirkland-Casgrain is the first woman in Quebec to sit in the provincial legislature.

1962 – 1975　　During this period, each province establishes comprehensive human rights legislation.

1964　　Married women in Quebec are given full legal rights.

1967　　The Royal Commission on the Status of Women in Canada is appointed.

　　　　　Brenda Robertson is the first woman elected to the New Brunswick legislature.

　　　　　Jean Gordon is the first woman elected to the Territorial Council of the Yukon Territory.

1969　　*Criminal Code* amendments legalize the sale of birth control devices and provide for legal abortions where a therapeutic abortion committee determines that a woman's life or health is endangered.

1970　　The Report of the Royal Commission on the Status of Women in Canada recommends extensive changes to improve the status of women in Canada. When the Report is tabled, there is only one woman Member of Parliament.

　　　　　The federal Parliament passes the first legislation providing for paid maternity leave under the unemployment insurance program.

　　　　　Jean Canfield is the first woman elected to the Prince Edward Island legislature.

　　　　　Lena Pederson is the first woman elected to the Territorial Council of the Northwest Territories.

　　　　　The *War Measures Act* is invoked in response to the "October Crisis".

1971　　Victoria Constitutional Conference.

1972　　Report of the Special Joint Committee of the Senate and the House of Commons on the Constitution of Canada.

1973   The Supreme Court of Canada upholds the law removing Indian status from women who married non-Indian men, even though Indian men retained their status when they married non-Indian women. The case was argued (and lost) using the ineffective *Canadian Bill of Rights* (the *Lavell* case).

The Supreme Court of Canada rules against an Alberta ranch wife who claimed a half share in the ranch that she had helped build up and run because it was held in her husband's name (the *Murdoch* case). This case resulted in new (more equitable) matrimonial property legislation being introduced in most provinces.

1975   The *Quebec Charter of Human Rights and Freedoms* is passed.

1976   The Parti Québécois is elected.

1977   The Pepin-Robarts Task Force on Canadian Unity is appointed.

1978   The constitutional conference is held in Ottawa.

The Supreme Court of Canada rules that it is not sex discrimination to discriminate against a pregnant woman with respect to unemployment insurance benefits (the *Bliss* case).

1978 – 1990   Through a series of provincial laws, spousal immunity in tort law is abolished, allowing wives and husbands to sue one another for personal injury claims. (P.E.I. is the first province to do this and Alberta the last.)

1979   The First Ministers fail to reach agreement to transfer divorce jurisdiction to the provinces.

1980   The federal government proposes a charter of rights.

1981   A case brought before the United Nations Human Rights Committee challenges removal of Indian status from women marrying non-Indian men, and succeeds on the basis of cultural discrimination rather than sex discrimination (the *Lovelace* case).

The Supreme Court of Canada finds that there is a constitutional convention requiring a "substantial measure" of provincial consent to constitutional change (the *Patriation Reference* case).

With the November Accord, the federal government and all provinces except Quebec reach agreement on basic content.

The federal government ratifies the *International Convention on the Elimination of all Forms of Discrimination Against Women*.

1982 On April 17, the *Constitution Act, 1982* comes into effect (includes the *Canadian Charter of Rights and Freedoms*, with the exception of section 15).

The Supreme Court of Canada finds that Quebec does not have a right to a constitutional veto.

Madam Justice Bertha Wilson becomes the first woman ever appointed to the Supreme Court of Canada.

1983 "Sexual assault" replaces rape provisions in the *Criminal Code*. The recent complaint rule is removed for the new offence. "Rape shield" provisions are introduced, limiting questioning of sexual assault victims about sexual conduct with persons other than the accused. Marital rape becomes a crime.

1984 Jeanne Sauvé is the first woman to become Governor General of Canada.

1985 On April 17, section 15 of the Charter comes into force.

Section 12(1)(b) of the *Indian Act* is repealed, allowing First Nations women to marry non-Indian men without losing their Indian status.

Manitoba passes the first pay equity legislation in Canada.

1987 On April 30, the First Ministers' Conference at Meech Lake leads to an agreement, known as the Meech Lake Constitutional Accord, to amend the Constitution.

The second First Ministers' Conference, held at Langevin Block, Parliament Hill, approves final changes to the Meech Lake Accord.

The Yukon Territory *Human Rights Act* is passed.

1988 The Supreme Court of Canada rules that section 251 of the *Criminal Code*, which limited women's access to abortion, is unconstitutional because it violates women's right to life, liberty, and the security of the person within the meaning of section 7 of the Charter (the *Morgentaler* case).

1989 The first Supreme Court of Canada case to discuss the meaning of equality in section 15 of the Charter holds that the purpose of the equality section of the Charter is to alleviate disadvantage (the *Andrews* case).

The Supreme Court of Canada (in the *Brooks* case) over-rules *Bliss* (see 1978 above) by declaring that discrimination based on pregnancy is sex discrimination.

In the *Janzen* case, the Supreme Court of Canada holds that sexual harassment is sex discrimination.

1990 In June, the last round of Meech Lake discussion fails.

Audrey McLaughlin is elected leader of the federal New Democratic Party; she is the first woman elected as leader of a federal party.

Kim Campbell becomes the first woman to serve as federal Minister of Justice and Attorney General.

The Supreme Court of Canada holds that a battered woman may use the defence of self-defence if she kills her abusive spouse, even when her life is not immediately threatened (the *Lavallée* case).

1991 The report of the Citizens' Forum on National Unity is released. The federal government produces a new set of constitutional proposals.

Rita Johnston becomes the first woman premier when Bill Vander Zalm resigns in B.C. and she is named as his replacement.

"Rape shield" provisions are struck down by the Supreme Court of Canada (the *Seaboyer* case), prompting calls for reform of sexual assault legislation (see 1983).

Introduction

Why should women care about Canada's constitution? Do ordinary people need to concern themselves about a dry legal document? Isn't it mostly about laws that don't affect the average woman? How can constitutional words do anything to change the economic and social disadvantages that really concern most women in Canada?

In the past few years, heated debates about the *Canadian Charter of Rights and Freedoms*, Aboriginal self-government, the Meech Lake Accord, and Senate reform have pushed constitutional issues into the limelight. Many Canadians are realizing that the constitution is important and affects our economic and social well-being. However, women are also aware that the constitution-making process is one of the most male-dominated areas of public life. The constitution is a crucial arena where the decisions made by men change women's lives.

Consider, for instance, the issues surrounding pregnancy and childbirth. The Schachters, a married couple, were expecting a child.[1] For a number of reasons, they decided that it would work out best if the husband stayed home initially with the newborn child, while the wife returned to a job once she had recovered from childbirth. But the *Unemployment Insurance Act* allowed only a mother — not a father — to receive benefits. If the Schachters had been adopting a child, then either the father or the mother could have taken 15 weeks of benefits. This seemed inconsistent and unfair. So Shalom Schachter went to court, challenging the law under the equality rights section of the Charter, which is part of the constitution. LEAF (the Women's Legal Education and Action Fund) intervened in the case, arguing that birth parents and adoptive parents should have the same UIC benefits; either the mother or the father should be able to take 15 weeks of parental leave. This would be **in addition to**, not instead of, UIC maternity benefits, which are provided to give women time to recover from childbirth. The trial court agreed with Shalom Schachter, and so did the Federal Court of Appeal.[2] This case shows how the constitution, as interpreted by the courts, can change stereotypical ideas about childrearing. The assumption that mothers, and not fathers, should bear primary responsibility for a newborn was found to be unacceptable.

In another case involving childbirth, the constitution inspired the court to reach a conclusion it had avoided on an earlier occasion: that pregnancy discrimination is sex discrimination. Susan Brooks was working as a cashier at a Safeway supermarket.[3] She became pregnant. Although

Safeway had a good benefits package for its employees, the sickness and accident insurance plan excluded pregnant women for a 17-week period around the time of birth. This meant that during that time, no matter what the problem, whether it was related to pregnancy or not, Susan Brooks wasn't covered if she wasn't able to work because of sickness or accident. Even if she broke her leg, she couldn't claim accident benefits.

Susan Brooks's complaint under the *Manitoba Human Rights Act* eventually reached the Supreme Court of Canada (again with LEAF intervening). In the Supreme Court, Chief Justice Brian Dickson stated that "in distinguishing pregnancy from all other health-related reasons for not working, the plan imposes unfair disadvantages on pregnant women."[4] Then, in a unanimous decision, the Court ruled that discrimination on the basis of pregnancy is sex discrimination. That may sound pretty obvious, but as recently as 1978 the Supreme Court had reached the opposite conclusion in the *Bliss* case.[5] In that case, the Court decided that Stella Bliss had not been discriminated against because of her sex but because she was pregnant — as if pregnant men would run the same hazard. But in the *Brooks* case, the Court said:

> *Over ten years have elapsed since the decision in Bliss. During that time there have been profound changes in women's labour force participation. With the benefit of a decade of hindsight and ten years of experience with claims of human rights discrimination and jurisprudence arising therefrom, I am prepared to say that Bliss was wrongly decided or, in any event, that Bliss would not be decided now as it was decided then. Combining paid work with motherhood and accommodating the childbearing needs of working women are ever-increasing imperatives. That those who bear children and benefit society as a whole thereby should not be economically or socially disadvantaged seems to bespeak the obvious.*[6]

The difference between the two cases, *Bliss* and *Brooks*, was not just ten years. The other event that occurred between 1979 and 1989 was the proclamation of the equality provisions of the Charter and the recognition by the courts that human rights legislation has status as part of the constitution.

Negative examples of the impact of the constitution on women are also easy to find. A woman whose husband leaves her with their children may want to ask for maintenance for herself and for their children, as well as for the right to continue to live in the family home. Under our constitution, the federal and the provincial government each have jurisdiction over part of the issues involved. Moreover, each has its own court system. Because of the way the constitution divides responsibilities, a woman may have to go to two different courts, or go to the higher court, which is more expensive and may require her to hire a lawyer and travel away from her community to appear in court.

Or think about how representatives are elected to provincial/territorial and federal legislatures. There are very few women in the Parliament of Canada and in the provincial/territorial legislatures; women are severely under-represented in the sense that they make up at least half the population but hold a much smaller fraction of the seats. It would be possible to have an electoral system that ensured better representation of women. But the choice made in our constitution is to ensure only geographic representation — seats are divided among the provinces and territories or among geographic regions of a specific province or territory.

Because of the importance of constitutional issues in people's lives, and because women's perspective is often left out of discussions about these issues, we prepared this publication to provide basic information about the Canadian constitution. Here you will find out what a constitution is, what its role is, and how it reflects and influences a nation's values and culture. We then describe the Canadian constitution, its component parts and their particular relevance to women. How did our constitution come about? We'll review some history. And we'll consider where we are in terms of women's participation in constitutional issues. How might that change?

What is a Constitution?

> **This section will:**
> - provide a basic definition of the constitution of a nation, and describe some of the functions that constitutions serve
> - suggest some of the ways that the constitution forms part of Canadian culture and how its role in our culture might be changing.

If you have belonged to any kind of organized voluntary group, such as a community association, trade union, or service club, you are familiar with the idea of a constitution. In a voluntary association, the constitution sets out who may belong to the group, who the officers of the organization are and how they are elected, what their powers and responsibilities are, when meetings are held, who may vote at meetings, and so on. And it usually sets out the main purposes of the organization. When a group runs smoothly, the constitution is seldom referred to. Members of the group are aware of its general principles, but usually it becomes important only when there is a dispute within the organization. The rest of the time, the group just carries on, developing its own traditions and ways of doing things; these are not in the written constitution, but they are well understood and followed consistently by group members.

The constitution of a nation like Canada is similar in some ways to the constitution of a voluntary organization; a national constitution is also a collection of principles, contained in documents and unwritten traditions. (This is not to imply that a nation is like a voluntary organization, whose members agree to be bound by its constitution and bylaws. The source of state authority is a much-debated theoretical issue that we will not deal with here.) At the same time, a national constitution deals with many more people, more complex relationships, and the exercise of great power. A country's constitution can deal with these kinds of issues:

What the state can do to individuals:

How are crimes defined and who may be punished for them? Can someone be locked up and interrogated by the police without being charged with a crime? Who has the right to stay in the country and who may be deported? Can children be taken away from their parents by child welfare authorities under certain circumstances?

How different parts of the state work together:

Can immigration officials make up new rules, or do these have to come from the legislature? Can a judge decide that a law passed by the legislature will not be applied? If the nation's leader declares war, can that declaration be overridden by the legislature or the courts?

How the geographic divisions of the country work together:

Are there some issues that only the central government can deal with? Are there some that only the provincial or state governments can deal with? What about municipal governments — what are their powers? Which governments can collect taxes from which citizens?

How leaders are chosen and how they can be removed from office:

Who can vote? Who can run for office? What is the role of political parties? How is a government formed? How can a political leader be removed from office? How are judges chosen, and how are they accountable once appointed?

At a minimum, "the main service of a good constitution is to put obstacles in the way of bad government."[1] At a maximum, a constitution can also amount to "a political manifesto or creed or testament. As such, . . . it evokes the respect and affection and, indeed, obedience of the people in a way which no exclusively legal document can hope to do."[2]

The United Kingdom, the source of many of Canada's political structures, has no formal written constitution; the constitution is seen mainly as a way of setting the rules governing interaction among the different parts of the state. By contrast, the constitution of the United States has great symbolic importance. It expresses and is seen as standing for fundamental values such as individual liberty and freedom. In some ways, it is like a sacred document — its contents are beyond question, and it must be defended from attack.

In Canada, the constitution did not have much symbolic importance until the advent of the *Canadian Charter of Rights and Freedoms* in 1982. Before the Charter, the primary Canadian constitutional document was the *British North America Act* of 1867. It set out rules governing the relationship between parts of the state and dividing jurisdiction between the federal and provincial governments — a pragmatic, businesslike arrangement. Canadians were not even tempted to view the constitution as a sacred document, given its mundane contents. Unlike some other nations' constitutional documents, the *British North America Act* does not contain any resounding commitment to human rights or freedom, such as the well-known statement in the U.S. *Declaration of Independence*:

> We hold these truths to be self-evident, that all men are created equal, that they are endowed by their Creator with certain unalienable Rights, that among these are Life, Liberty and the pursuit of Happiness.

The drafters of the *British North America Act* directed their efforts not to the rights or freedoms of citizens but to "the Welfare of the Provinces" and the promotion of "the Interests of the British Empire". The closest they came to a statement of principle was the phrase "Peace, Order and Good Government", which is used to describe the legislative powers of the federal government.

The differences between the U.S. and Canadian constitutions stem from their different histories of separation from the United Kingdom. In the United States, the constitution was the outcome of a long struggle, culminating in the Revolutionary War and a new beginning in the name of "We, The People".[3] Canada's constitution was the outcome of occasional spirited rebellions and a long process of incremental change, but not revolution.[4] To explain the lack of cultural and symbolic meaning in the *British North America Act*, political scientist Alan Cairns has written:

> *A partial explanation is found in the nature of the British North America Act. It is a document of monumental dullness which enshrines no eternal principles and is devoid of inspirational content. It was not born in a revolutionary, populist context, and it acquired little symbolic aura in its subsequent history. The movement to Confederation was not a rejection of Europe, but was rather a pragmatic response to a series of economic, political, military, and technological considerations. There was no need for the kind of political theorizing that accompanied the American experience of creating a new political entity and exercised a spell on subsequent generations.*[5]

Consistent with this history, constitutional change in Canada has always been a top-down process, as opposed to one that invites public participation.[6]

The cultural significance of our constitution has increased since 1982 for several reasons. The absence of Quebec as a partner to the 1982 constitutional amendments, the 1983 Constitutional Accord on Aboriginal Rights, and a growing awareness of Aboriginal issues and their relationship to the constitution have contributed dramatically to the profile of the constitution in Canadian society. The struggle of women and other disadvantaged groups for a broad and meaningful interpretation of Canadian Charter equality rights has also played an important role. This new view of the constitution is illustrated by the comment of Ethel Blondin, MP: "The constitution is like a mirror. You should see some reflection of yourself when you look at it."[7]

Discussion Questions

1. What is a constitution? What would you identify as the most important function of a constitution?

2. Identify some common features of a country's constitution? What would you include?

3. How does Canada's constitution differ from that of the United Kingdom? United States? other countries?

4. Do you think the way we look at our constitution has changed? Has its role in our daily lives increased? How?

What is a Feminist Perspective?

> **This section will:**
> - identify three elements in a feminist perspective on the constitution — recognizing that our constitution is "man-made"; that constitutional principles must reflect the needs and interests of all women; and that the constitution must be viewed in a social context in which women are devalued
> - illustrate the impact on women of the relationship between our constitution and social change.

So far, what we have said about constitutions is what you might find in any textbook on the subject. We want to do more than that; we want to look at constitutions — especially the Canadian constitution — from a feminist perspective.

What does it mean to take a feminist perspective on the constitution?

First, it means recognizing that the principles of the constitution were not put there by God or some force of nature. Over time, and through a complex process, economically privileged, white, able-bodied Christian men formulated the Canadian constitution. Historically, women have had almost no input. The constitution in Canadian society, and in the French and English societies from which our own constitution derived, is overwhelmingly man-made.

Second, a feminist perspective means valuing women's needs and interests as highly as those of men. Because the Canadian constitution reflects the needs and interests of the men who made it, and not necessarily those of women, its principles are open to question. A feminist perspective avoids the error of equating "masculine" with "human" and seeks to correct situations where that error has occurred. In taking a feminist perspective, it is also important to avoid the error of equating the experiences of white, relatively privileged, able-bodied women with those of all women. Thus, if the selection and formulation of the core principles of the Canadian constitution don't reflect the needs and interests of **all** women, those principles are open to question.

Third, a feminist perspective means seeing the constitution in context. Our constitution exists in a society, and is expressed in a language, in which women are devalued. The constitution expresses an elite male view of what is important and, by expressing it, helps to make it so. Changing constitutional wording does not necessarily bring about social change. Nor does social change always require constitutional amendment. Nevertheless, they are often closely related.

A vivid example illustrates this point. When the *British North America Act* was written in 1867 by the "Fathers of Confederation", it provided that qualified "persons" could be named to the Senate by the Governor General. Sixty years later, no woman had yet been appointed. Emily Murphy, an Edmonton magistrate, launched a campaign to change that. In 1919, as the first president of the Federated Women's Institutes of Canada, she got unanimous support to call for the appointment of a woman senator. The National Council of Women and the Montreal Women's Club passed similar resolutions, naming Murphy herself as their nominee. After eight years of trying and getting nowhere, Emily Murphy used an obscure provision in the *Supreme Court Act*. Along with four suffragist colleagues from Alberta, she requested a constitutional interpretation of just who were "persons" under the *British North America Act*.[1] The Court ruled unanimously: men only. The women appealed to the British Privy Council, which overturned the earlier decision and ruled in favour of Murphy and her colleagues.[2] This has come to be known as the "Persons Case".

The Persons Case highlights how things change over time. In 1927, the Supreme Court of Canada assumed (probably rightly) that in 1867 the Fathers of Confederation would never have contemplated such a radical step as considering women to be "persons" for the purpose of holding public office. The case brought before the Court in 1927 asserted that women have as valuable a contribution to make to public life as men do, and that women's needs and interests should be recognized. The Supreme Court chose a conservative interpretation, faithful to its forefathers of sixty years earlier. But the final decision by the British Privy Council was not dictated by constitutional wording or legal niceties; rather, it reflected the judges' recognition that social change in the role of women now qualified them for consideration as potential senators. The Privy Council recognized in 1930 that the issue was not so much why women should be included but why they should not.[3] (This was echoed, 45 years later, in Canada's slogan for International Women's Year: "Why not?") Significantly, the Privy Council said that the constitution should be viewed as "a living tree capable of growth and expansion within its natural limits."[4] In other words, whatever the Fathers of Confederation might have thought about women in public office in 1867, the Privy Council said the issue should be determined in the social context of 1930, when the case was decided. The slowness with which constitutional change leads to social change is evident in the low numbers of women in Parliament more than 60 years after the *Persons* Case — 40 of 295 or 13.5 per cent in the House of Commons and 15 of 103 or 14.6 per cent in the Senate.

Discussion Questions

1. What do you think it means to have a feminist perspective on the constitution?

2. How can a constitution service the needs and interests of all women?

What is the Canadian Constitution?

This section is divided into two parts: (1) a description of Canada's formal constitutional documents and conventions, and (2) a review of some important principles found in both the written and unwritten parts of our constitution.

> **Part 1 will:**
>
> - identify entrenched and supreme constitutional documents, such as the *Canada Act, 1982*, and other constitutional documents which are not entrenched, such as the *Supreme Court Act*;
> - discuss the limitations and importance of unwritten constitutional rules or conventions

Where is the Constitution Found?

In addition to the Canadian constitution, each province has its own constitution. We will discuss only the national constitution. It is found in both formal documents and in "conventions" (practices and traditions).

Formal Documents

It may come as a surprise, but there is no single all-inclusive document that we can identify as the constitution of Canada. Instead, there is an assortment of Canadian constitutional documents that fall into two main categories.

1. The listed documents — entrenched and supreme

A number of documents are listed in the definition of the "Constitution of Canada" in the *Constitution Act, 1982*. These cannot be changed except by special constitutional amendment, so they are said to be "entrenched". They are placed above all other laws in Canada and are therefore said to be "supreme". Here are the listed documents:[1]

(a) *Canada Act, 1982*. This is the law passed by the Parliament of the United Kingdom in 1982, as a result of the agreement between the government of Canada and the governments of all provinces except Quebec. It enacts the *Constitution Act, 1982*, which sets out a procedure for amending the Canadian constitution in Canada. It also includes the *Canadian Charter of Rights and Freedoms*. The *Canada Act, 1982* was the law that was said to have "patriated" the Canadian constitution; it ended the right of the Parliament of the United Kingdom to pass any more legislation effective in Canada, including legislation amending the constitution. (The Charter, the newest part of the constitution, is discussed in much greater detail later on.)

(b) *Constitution Act, 1867*, formerly called the *British North America Act*, and its amendments. This law, passed by the Parliament of the United Kingdom in 1867, brought about the Confederation of the original four provinces of Canada. It divided legislative jurisdiction (that is, who has the right to pass laws about particular subjects) between federal and provincial governments; provided for the entry of additional provinces; and dealt with numerous other issues. (This Act is discussed in more detail in the historical review that follows and in the description of the division of powers.)

(c) Various laws admitting provinces or territories to Confederation or altering boundaries. (These are not discussed in this publication.)

(d) *Statute of Westminster, 1931*. This law limited the power of the Parliament of the United Kingdom to pass laws for dominions such as Canada and Australia. But constitutional amendments for Canada still had to be made through acts of the imperial Parliament of the United Kingdom. (This statute is referred to briefly in the historical section on the evolution of the constitution.)

2. The unlisted documents

The second category consists of numerous documents not listed in the *Constitution Act, 1982*, including the *Royal Proclamation of 1763*,[2] the *Quebec Act of 1774*, the *Constitutional Act of 1791*, and the *Supreme Court Act*. These documents are neither "entrenched" nor "supreme"; however, this does not mean that they are referred to as "the fundamental document setting out the basis of Indian-European relations",[3] and as having "status analogous to [the] Magna Carta."[4]

Conventions

A well-established set of rules — called "conventions" — governs many aspects of our constitutional life. These conventions could have been written down and included in the formal documents, but they have not been. Instead, they have the status of "non-legal rules".[5] They are extremely important, because they prescribe how legal powers are exercised. The Supreme Court of Canada explained it this way in the *Patriation Reference* case:

> *The main purpose of constitutional conventions is to ensure that the legal framework of the Constitution will be operated in accordance with the prevailing constitutional values or principles of the period.*[6]

Here are two important examples of constitutional conventions:

1. *Responsible government*

"Responsible government" refers to the British-style system where the prime minister and cabinet are elected members of the House of Commons; they form a government and hold office as long as the House of Commons continues to have confidence in them. Nothing in the formal constitutional documents refers to "responsible government". However, the preamble to the *Constitution Act, 1867* states that the four provinces had "expressed their Desire to be federally united into One Dominion under the Crown of the United Kingdom of Great Britain and Ireland, with a Constitution similar in Principle to that of the United Kingdom." Because the United Kingdom's constitution embodies principles of responsible government, those principles (by convention and tradition) are an essential part of the Canadian constitution as well.

2. *Governor General acts on advice of the government*

If you read only the formal documents of our constitution, you might think that the Governor General, appointed by the monarch, has extensive and sweeping powers. But of course, this conclusion would be wrong. By convention, the Governor General exercises her/his powers only at the request of the prime minister or the cabinet. This includes even specific powers, such as the power of the Governor General or the Queen to withhold royal assent from legislation that has been passed by both houses of Parliament. A convention dictates that royal assent shall never be withheld.

Constitutional conventions are not enforced by the courts. But they have been recognized by the courts in some situations. One of the most important was in 1981, in the *Patriation Reference* case. The federal government proposed to ask the Parliament of the United Kingdom to amend the Canadian constitution in a way that would affect provincial powers. Some of the provinces said there was a convention, or even a legal rule, against the federal government acting in that way without the consent of the provinces. In its decision, the Supreme Court of Canada made it clear that the Canadian constitution consists of both constitutional law and constitutional conventions. It said there was a constitutional convention (but not a legal rule) requiring a "substantial measure" of provincial consent to such amendments.

The *Patriation Reference* case illustrates both the limitations and the importance of conventions. Because the rule requiring a substantial measure of provincial consent was a convention and not a legal rule, the Supreme Court could not enforce it. The federal government could have gone ahead with its proposal without breaking the law. But because the political consequences would have been enormous, the federal government went back to the bargaining table with the provinces. Eventually, nine of the ten provinces (the exception being Quebec) agreed with the proposed resolution. Later, in a case brought by the province of Quebec, the Supreme Court of Canada held that the consent of Quebec was not necessary to comply with the convention,[7] thus legally validating the *Constitution Act, 1982*.

Why have such important conventions never been written down or become part of formal constitutional documents? This has certainly been discussed, especially before the 1982 constitutional reform. It is likely that the conventions were not incorporated into the formal constitution because many are controversial and some would be difficult to state clearly and concisely in language everyone could agree on. The level of agreement necessary to put them into the written constitution would have been very difficult to achieve in 1981-82, and no less difficult today. On the plus side, the conventions bring a measure of flexibility to our constitutional system. As the late Eugene Forsey argued:

> *The "silences" of our written Constitution are, in fact, one of its greatest glories. They leave us room to adapt, to innovate, to experiment, to grow; room for Borden's "exercise of the commonplace quality of common sense."*[8]

On the other hand, as feminists (naturally sceptical about what can sound like "gentlemen's agreements") and as citizens, we may feel some unease about the magnitude of what is left unclear in the constitution.

Discussion Questions

Part 1: Where is the Constitution found?

1. What are Canada's constitutional documents and conventions?

2. Does the flexibility provided by general statements of principle and/or unwritten conventions work for or against women and other disadvantaged groups?

What are the Important Principles of Canada's Constitution?

Now that we know that Canada's constitutional principles can be found in both formal documents and conventions, the next question is, what are those principles? In Part 2, we outline some of the most important ones.

Part 2 will:

- identify fundamental constitutional principles including those defining the role of the Crown, the three branches of government (legislative, executive, and judicial), the division of powers between the federal and provincial government, constitutional amending processes, and the rights and freedoms guaranteed under the *Canadian Charter of Rights and Freedoms*;
- discuss the representation of women as Canada's heads of state, in the Cabinet, in the Senate and House of Commons, on the bench and in the legal profession, and in the federal public service;
- briefly review the barriers to women's participation in public life in Canada and discuss whether having more women in all of the institutions identified above would make a difference;
- identify the concept of territoriality and control as central to the division of powers between the federal and provincial governments, briefly outline the division of powers and discuss the impact of this division on the lives of women in areas such as family law and social programs;
- identify the various mechanisms for amending Canada's constitution;
- outline the structure of the *Canadian Charter of Rights and Freedoms*, with examples of its impact on women drawn from court cases and constitutional debate;
- identify four categories of rights and freedoms in the Canadian Charter, describing how these affect women and other disadvantaged groups with examples drawn from abortion, hate laws, sexual assault, pregnancy discrimination, sexual harassment, and collective rights relating to language, Aboriginal peoples, and multicultural interests;
- identify some issues not dealt with in the Charter, such as social rights to such basics as nourishment, shelter, medical assistance, and education.

The Crown

The Queen is Canada's head of state. Her representatives, the Governor General of Canada and the Lieutenant Governors of the provinces, possess considerable power in theory but virtually none in practice. It has been argued that responsible government is unworkable without a formal head of state with the power to ensure that governments don't overstep their bounds or that some form of order remains even if a government falls.[9] For example, Canada's Governor General can dismiss a prime minister who refuses to resign or call an election after losing the confidence of the legislature. If there were no such power, legislative stalemates could occur, with the risk that people might attempt to resolve them outside the law. Another advantage of having a formal head of state separate from the political leader is that this may help to diffuse the power concentrated in one person. The public adulation of the president of the United States, which sometimes seems excessive to Canadians, might be lessened if the president were not both head of government and head of state. Queens have been Canada's heads of state for 73 of the 124 years since Confederation, thus placing women in this symbolic position.[10] There has been one female Governor General in Canadian history, the Right Honourable Jeanne Sauvé.

The Branches of Government

The constitution establishes three branches of government: legislative, executive, and judicial. Their functions are related but distinct.

1. The legislative branch

Laws are created in two ways: by judges, through the "common law" process, and by legislatures, through legislation. The legislative branch at the federal level is Parliament, which includes the Queen, the Senate, and the House of Commons. The House of Commons is elected by citizens over the age of 18 (although voters can be disqualified under certain circumstances). The Senate is appointed by the Governor General (upon the recommendation of the federal cabinet). Legislation must be passed by both the House of Commons and the Senate. Although occasionally the Senate will stall legislation, the prevailing view is that, because the Senate is appointed rather than elected, it should defer to the will of the elected representatives in the House of Commons. Representation of women in Parliament has increased very slowly. [Editorial note: As this manuscript goes to press (August 1992), 40 women sit in the House of Commons (13.5 per cent of the 295 MPs), and there are 15 women Senators (14.6 per cent of the 103 Senators)].

2. The executive branch

The executive branch consists of the prime minister and the cabinet (by convention, since neither the prime minister nor the cabinet is mentioned in the *Constitution Act, 1867*). The Governor General "chooses" the prime minister, but by convention must select someone who can form a government with the confidence of the House of Commons. This means that the Governor General calls upon the leader of the political party that holds a majority of seats in the House of Commons. Where there is no party with a majority of seats, the Governor General usually calls on the leader of the party with the best chance of maintaining a stable minority government. The prime minister then chooses a cabinet and informs the Governor General who, by convention, appoints those persons as ministers of the Crown. Again by convention, cabinet ministers must be members of Parliament (from the House of Commons or the Senate) when appointed or they must become members as soon as possible.

The cabinet has the executive authority to set the legislative agenda for Parliament and is responsible for the administration of all government departments.[11] The actual work of developing, administering, and implementing government policy is done by public servants, who may exercise a great deal of informal authority. Women are well represented in the lower levels of the public service (for example, in clerical jobs), but are not well represented at higher levels. In a recent report documenting the barriers to women in the federal public service, the writers concluded:

We have established that women in the federal public service are compressed into low levels of pay and status and confined to a few large occupational groups that provide poor access to promotion; that they advance in relatively frequent small increments starting from low levels and moving within occupational groups rather than across them; that if nothing changes, it could be another half century before anything approaching equity is achieved and that women do perceive gender-based barriers to advancement in the federal public service and can describe them clearly.[12]

Political scientist Sylvia Bashevkin points out the significance of the absence of women from the upper ranks of the public service:

. . . high-ranking public servants in Canada would appear to exercise greater policy influence than most legislators, and probably some cabinet ministers. This pattern suggests that electing more women to the pinnacle of legislative office, the House of Commons, may prove futile in policy terms unless attention is given at the same time to recruiting females to senior-level bureaucratic positions, particularly within central agencies of the federal government.[13]

Informally, the prime minister exercises a great deal of authority. Peter Hogg has observed:

Criticism of the "imperial presidency" occasionally conveys the impression that the President of the United States is a more powerful figure within the American presidential system of government than is the Prime Minister (or provincial Premier) within a system of responsible government. This is incorrect. In a normal situation of majority government, the Prime Minister's leadership of the majority party in the House of Commons, reinforced by strict party discipline, and sanctioned by his power to dissolve the House, leads to a concentration of power in the hands of the Prime Minister that has no counterpart in the presidential (or gubernatorial) system.[14]

By custom, the prime minister also acts as the convener and chair of first ministers' conferences. This position enhances the power of the prime minister. The practice of "executive federalism", whereby important inter-governmental issues, including constitutional changes, are dealt with at closed meetings of the eleven first ministers (the prime minister and ten provincial premiers), increases the power of all eleven participants.

Until deputy premier Rita Johnston was named to replace Bill Vander Zalm in the spring of 1991, as premier of British Columbia, there had never been a woman prime minister or premier. Audrey McLaughlin, the current leader of the New Democratic Party, is the first woman to be elected leader of a federal political party; and only a few women have been leaders of major provincial parties.

Representation of women in the federal cabinet reached a high of 6 out of 39 in 1989 (15.4 per cent). The emphasis on "leadership" during election campaigns works against women's participation in politics because "leadership qualities" are usually viewed as those stereotypically identified with men: toughness, firmness, the ability to dominate.[15] Many women do, in fact, possess those qualities. But more important, the leadership shown by people with these qualities is not the only kind of leadership, nor is it necessarily the best kind of leadership.

3. The judicial branch

The judicial branch consists of the various courts that consider legal disputes. Judges are responsible for defining the common law and interpreting statutes. Common law is the body of judge-made law that is used, for example, when one person sues another for damages because of a broken contract or a broken leg. Statutes are the laws passed by legislatures. Diagram A, depicting the Canadian court system, shows that there are two courts at the national level: the Supreme Court of Canada and the Federal Court of Canada.

The Supreme Court of Canada was established in 1875 and became Canada's court of final resort in 1949.[16] Nine judges are appointed to that court on the recommendation of the federal cabinet. Three of the Supreme Court judges must come from Quebec, and there are conventions that three must also come from Ontario, two from the western provinces, and one from the Atlantic provinces. As well, there is a practice of alternating the position of Chief Justice between francophones and anglophones. The first woman (Madam Justice Bertha Wilson) was appointed to the Supreme Court of Canada in 1982; there are now two women on the court (Madam Justice Claire L'Heureux-Dubé and Madam Justice Beverley McLachlin). Often (but not always) all nine Supreme Court justices hear an appeal together.

As the court of final resort for all provinces, the Supreme Court is at the top of the hierarchy of all courts in Canada. It hears appeals on a very limited number of cases, which may be civil, criminal, or purely constitutional.[17] While it can overrule itself, and has done so on a few occasions, no other court can overrule its decisions. Further, courts below it are bound to follow its decisions where applicable. In many instances, however, Supreme Court decisions can be overruled by Parliament or the provincial legislatures. This is because of the constitutional tradition of parliamentary supremacy. (The effect of the *Canadian Charter of Rights and Freedoms* on the ability of legislatures to have the last word is discussed below.)

A unique feature of the Canadian constitutional system is the "reference case". The *Supreme Court Act* provides for the Supreme Court to give advisory opinions to the federal government upon request. These opinions are rarely sought except in constitutional cases, for example, the Persons Case concerning the eligibility of women to be senators. Provincial legislation also allows for those governments to seek similar opinions from the provincial appellate courts.[18]

Diagram A

The Canadian Judicial System

The Supreme Court of Canada✤

Nine judges are appointed to the Supreme Court. The court hears appeals from Provincial Courts of Appeal, the Federal Court of Appeal, and references from the federal government.

Provincial Courts of Appeal✤

Such as the British Columbia Court of Appeal, the Prince Edward Island Supreme Court Appeal Division, and the Ontario Court of Appeal. These courts hear appeals from lower courts and references from the provincial government.

Federal Court of Appeal✤

This court hears appeals from the Federal Court, Trial Division, as well as appeals from certain administrative tribunals such as the Immigration Appeal Board.

Provincial Trial Courts✤

Such as the Alberta Court of Queen's Bench, the British Columbia Supreme Court, and the Ontario Court of Justice (General Division). These courts hear civil and criminal cases and some appeals from the Provincial Courts.

Federal Court, Trial Division✤

This court hears cases where the federal government is a party and with respect to certain matters under federal jurisdiction, i.e., immigration, income tax, unemployment insurance, and appeals from other federal administrative agencies.

Provincial Courts✤✤

Such as the British Columbia Provincial Court, the Cour du Québec (Chambre civile and Chambre Criminelle et Pénale), and the Ontario Court of Justice (Provincial Division). These courts hear less serious and preliminary criminal cases, small claims, cases concerning the protection of children, and other family law matters.*

✤ Denotes a section 96 court. The judges are appointed by the federal government.

✤✤ Judges in Provincial Courts are appointed by the provincial government.

* Nova Scotia also has a County Court which hears some civil and many criminal cases. Some provinces also have Probate or Surrogate Courts.

The Federal Court of Canada has jurisdiction over certain matters under federal law, such as income tax, immigration, and unemployment insurance cases. Its judges also are appointed by the federal government. It has a trial and an appeals division. The need for a separate Federal Court has frequently been debated. Many argue that it would be much more efficient to have the superior courts of the provinces deal with these areas of law.

The federal government has also constituted and appoints judges to the territorial courts in the Northwest Territories and the Yukon.[19]

Finally, the federal government makes appointments to the provincial superior courts, which include appeal courts and trial courts in each province. Like the Supreme Court of Canada and the Federal Court of Appeal, the provincial appeal courts delegate three or more judges to hear each case. The trial courts are usually called "Queen's Bench" or "Supreme Court". For a case heard at the trial level, only one judge sits on the bench.

The courts described so far are sometimes referred to as the "section 96 courts", since it is under section 96 of the *Constitution Act, 1867* that the federal government has authority to appoint judges to them.

The "provincial" courts are another level of court. These are constituted by provincial governments, and judges are appointed to them by provincial cabinets. Provincial court judges hear less serious or preliminary criminal cases, certain family law matters, and some civil disputes where a lesser amount of money is involved.

Judges are no longer appointed for life, but section 96 judges may stay in office until the age of 75 unless removed from office for grave misconduct.[20] While it is true that, once appointed, judges are independent of government, the government does influence the judiciary through its selection of those who are appointed. There has always been an element of political patronage in judicial appointments.[21] As well, judges are appointed from the ranks of the legal profession, so they come from a relatively privileged background. While judges are expected to be above partisan politics, it is obvious that the life experiences and "small-p" political perspective of judges can affect how they decide cases.

There are many examples of this. An obvious one is found from the time when women were attempting to gain entry to the professions. In 1915, Annie Macdonald Langstaff petitioned the Quebec Superior Court to allow her to take the preliminary bar examination for entry to the legal profession. Mr. Justice Saint-Pierre, refusing her petition, said:

I would put within the range of possibilities though by no means a commendable one, the admission of a woman to the profession of solicitor or to that of avoué, but I hold that to admit a woman and more particularly a married woman as a barrister, that is to say, as a person who pleads cases at the bar before judges or juries in open court and in the presence of the public, would be nothing short of a direct infringement upon public order and a manifest violation of the law of good morals and public decency.

Let us for a moment picture to ourselves a woman appearing as defending or prosecuting counsel in a case of rapt (sic) [rape] and putting to the complainant the questions which must of all necessity be asked in order to make proof of the acts which are of the essence of the crime or which are equally necessary to meet and repeal the charge.

No woman possessing the least sense of decency could possibly do so without throwing a blur upon her own dignity and without bringing into utter contempt the honor and respect due to her sex.[22]

Until very recently, there were few women judges. During the Mulroney government's first term of office, 17.8 per cent of its judicial appointments were women.[23] Even so, the percentage of female superior court judges across Canada remains very low — less than 9 per cent overall.

4. How the three branches of government fit together

As might be imagined, the three branches do not always fit together smoothly. For one thing, many of the rules about the powers and responsibilities of the different branches are found in convention rather than in a written code, so the lines are not always clearly drawn. The principles, however, are depicted in Diagram B.

At the top of the diagram is the head of state: the Queen or her representatives, the Governor General or Lieutenant Governors. Under responsible government (which, as described above, exists almost entirely by convention), the head of state must act under the direction or "advice" of the prime minister and cabinet (the executive branch). The executive stays in office only as long as it enjoys the confidence of a majority of the **elected** members of the House of Commons (the legislative branch).

Legislation is usually initiated by the executive branch. It must be voted on by the House of Commons, then the Senate, and becomes law following signature by the head of state. It is then implemented by the public service, under the direction of the executive branch.

The judicial branch operates under statutes passed by the legislative branch, which also approves funding for the courts. Judges are appointed by the executive branch. Once appointed, however, judges are expected and entitled to be independent of the political process.[24] Chief justices or judges of the Supreme Court of Canada on some occasions represent the head of state. This is an historical relic of the fact that English judges sat in court as representatives of the monarch.

5. Women's participation

A common feature of all three branches of government is the small number of women. Initially, there were formal barriers to women's participation, such as the exclusion of women

Diagram B

Branches of Government

Head of State

The Queen and the Governor-General

The Head of State acts on the advice of the Executive Branch.

Legislative Branch

Parliament (The Queen, the Senate, and the House of Commons).

The political party which holds the majority of seats in the House of Commons forms the government. Both the House of Commons and the Senate must approve all legislation. Senators are appointed by the Prime Minister. Senators, unlike the members of the House of Commons, are not elected.

Executive Branch

The Prime Minister and the Cabinet.

The members of the Executive Branch are drawn from the political party which forms the government in the House of Commons. The Executive Branch sets the legislative agenda for Parliament and is responsible for the administration of all government departments.

The Public Service is the arm of the Executive Branch responsible for the actual implementation and administration of government policy.

Judicial Branch

The Courts of Law.

The courts are funded by the Legislative Branch. Judicial appointments are made by the Executive Branch. The Judicial Branch develops the common law, interprets statutes, and decides on the constitutionality of challenged legislation.

from voting, running for public office, holding public service jobs after marriage, entering the legal profession, or sitting as judges or jurors. But now, despite the removal of the legal barriers, government institutions are still largely male. In many ways, in fact, our institutions don't reflect the diversity of the population as a whole. And the higher we look, the worse it gets. For example, there has never been a non-white first minister or Supreme Court of Canada justice. The first ministers' conferences are the epitome of unrepresentativeness. To this date, they have been 100 per cent male and white, able-bodied, aged between 40 and 65, and almost invariably Christian.

Would having more women in the legislatures, in cabinet, in the public service, and the judiciary make a difference? Obviously, the likelihood that women's interests would be overlooked or denigrated would be reduced (although not necessarily eliminated). Moreover, the appearance of government would change, leading more women to see themselves as involved in the process and, perhaps, to expect and demand more from it.

Taking the judicial branch as an example, Madam Justice Bertha Wilson of the Supreme Court of Canada has said that more women judges make a difference, simply by seeing the world through different eyes.[25] The decision of the Supreme Court of Canada in the *Lavallée* case[26] illustrates this point. Lyn Lavallée was charged with the murder of her common-law husband. She pleaded self-defence. Her lawyer argued that Ms. Lavallée's history of being battered by her husband affected her when she fired the gun that killed him. A psychiatrist gave evidence about the general effects of persistent battering on women and why many women stay in such relationships. The Court reviewed and revised some existing criminal law principles and decided that Ms. Lavallée could claim self-defence because she had suffered persistent physical abuse, even though she shot her common-law husband at a moment when he was not actually attacking her. This decision recognized that the law of self-defence was written to deal with typically male experiences (such as bar-room brawls), not to deal with typically female experiences (such as the spouse trapped in an abusive relationship). Of the six judges who signed the majority decision written by Madam Justice Wilson, three were women.

The importance of increasing women's participation in all aspects of government is evident. It does not need to be justified on the indefensible ground that all women see the world the same way, or that all women see the world differently from all men. Such generalizations are both unprovable and dangerous. Instead, it can be justified on these grounds:

1. those who are subject to the laws should be represented in the institutions that formulate, enact, and enforce the laws;

2. women tend to have life experiences that men do not share, both because our society treats women and men differently, and because women become pregnant and give birth (thus, for example, women have a much greater chance of living in poverty as single parents); and

3. without role models, young women will not aspire to political office, the judiciary, or managerial jobs, and the exclusion of women will be perpetuated.

Division of Powers

1. The concept

The division of powers between federal and provincial governments is so much a part of the Canadian constitutional landscape that it is difficult to stand back far enough to question it. But this scheme, like all human systems, tells a great deal about the people who created it and the circumstances in which they lived.

The constitutions of some countries are unitary, that is, the constitution provides for a single central government whose law-making powers are supreme throughout the country. The United Kingdom and New Zealand provide examples of unitary constitutions. On the other hand, some countries (such as Canada, the United States, and Australia) have adopted federal constitutions. In a federal constitution, there are usually two levels of government: a central government with authority over the whole country for some matters, and independent state or provincial governments with authority over other matters in their states or provinces. The second type of government is not subordinate to the central government. State or provincial governments are autonomous within their designated areas.

When the provinces of Canada West (Ontario), Canada East (Quebec), Nova Scotia, and New Brunswick negotiated the terms of confederation in 1867, the document recording those terms (the *British North America Act*, now called the *Constitution Act, 1867*) created a federal rather than a unitary state. The participants wanted to build a strong central government while preserving regional and cultural autonomy. There were important and well-established differences among the provinces that made a unitary state impossible. Yet some favoured that option, particularly in Ontario. Sir John A. Macdonald, who supported a unitary state, had to accept the federal model, but he did succeed in getting a constitution tilted toward strong central government.[27]

By contrast, the U.S. constitution was tilted initially toward strong state government. The fact that Canada's constitution now tends toward strong provincial government and the U.S. constitution toward central government shows that constitutional wording is not the final determinant of constitutional behaviour. The way governments act and the way courts interpret constitutional wording can lead to the evolution of arrangements very different from those originally intended.

Underlying the concept of division of powers between federal and provincial governments in Canada's constitution are notions of territoriality and control. As feminists, we see a possible connection between this and historical patterns of male behaviour reflecting a need for territorial dominance. The division-of-powers model reflects not just where and when the Fathers of Confederation lived, and the geographic and cultural diversity of the places they represented, but also who they were. This highlights the fact that there are other ways of doing things besides the one that happens to have been chosen for us more than a century ago.

2. Implementation

Under the *Constitution Act, 1867*, section 91 lists the areas where the federal government has the authority to make laws, while section 92 describes the areas under provincial authority. The federal government can make laws "for the Peace, Order, and good Government of Canada" in all matters not assigned exclusively to the provinces. In addition to that general power, Parliament has sole control over a number of other matters, including the military, the postal service, the regulation of trade and commerce, the census, the public debt, weights and measures, interest rates, banks and currency, navigation and shipping, criminal law, copyrights and patents, "Indians, and Lands reserved for the Indians", and "Naturalization and Aliens".

In section 92, provinces are given jurisdiction over a different list: reformatory prisons, the management of hospitals, asylums and charities, municipal institutions, "Local Works and Undertakings", "Property and Civil Rights in the Province", and a number of other areas of local interest or concerning the administration of government in the provinces. Section 93 gives the provinces exclusive jurisdiction over education, subject to the provisions for denominational schools included at that time.

Each level of government has the power to raise revenue through taxes,[28] and Parliament and the provincial legislatures share jurisdiction over the legal system.[29] Jurisdiction over the export of natural resources, old age pensions, immigration, and agriculture is concurrent, meaning that both levels of government may legislate in the area.[30]

Language was not one of the areas divided between the two levels of government in 1867. The *British North America Act* did require that both languages be permitted in Parliament, in the Quebec legislature, and in the federal and Quebec courts, and that federal and Quebec statutes be published in both languages. This provision was later extended to Manitoba when it joined Confederation in 1870.[31] Linguistic and religious concerns were addressed indirectly by assigning control over education to the provinces, along with the promise that existing separate school systems would be maintained.[32]

Similarly, some areas of social law and policy that have since become important were not even contemplated in 1867. These were added later: unemployment insurance in 1940[33] and old age pensions and disability benefits in 1964.[34] Although these programs would normally fall under provincial jurisdiction, through constitutional amendment they were created as national programs. Technological advances have also required new interpretations. Judicial decisions have determined, for example, that regulation of aeronautics is within federal authority because of the peace, order, and good government power.[35]

There has never been an area of jurisdiction called "Provisions for Sex Equality", or any debate about whether there should be one and, if so, whether it should fall under federal, provincial, or joint jurisdiction. Issues involving sex equality fall under federal or provincial jurisdiction depending on the context in which they arise. For example, both provincial and federal governments have passed human rights laws to prohibit discrimination in employment. Which laws apply in a given case? It depends whether the employer is operating under federal or provincial authority. Federal authority includes the federal public service, Crown corporations, navigation and shipping, interprovincial transportation, and communication. In all other cases, because the regulation of labour relations falls under "property and civil rights in the province", provincial laws apply.

The courts adjudicate "boundary disputes" between federal and provincial governments. For example, criminal law is assigned to the federal government. If a province passes legislation that a court considers to be criminal law, that legislation will be struck down as unconstitutional.[36] In this way, Canada's constitution is different from that of the United Kingdom, where the courts do not review laws. Until 1982 it was also different from the U.S. constitution, which invites review of legislation for conformity with fundamental rights and freedoms as well as for conformity with jurisdictional rules. Only with the introduction of the Charter were the Canadian courts given the wider powers of review that they now possess.

Sometimes, federal and provincial laws exist in the same area. For example, there may be a criminal law against soliciting and a municipal bylaw (under provincial authority) against creating a nuisance. What happens if both laws are constitutionally sound but they conflict or are inconsistent with one another? The rule known as "federal paramountcy" dictates that the federal law prevails.

Over the years, federal and provincial governments have been able to compromise when faced with disputes over jurisdiction. Unemployment insurance and social benefits programs, mentioned earlier, are two examples. One of the main ways to reach compromise has been the federal-provincial conference, where the first ministers or ministers responsible for particular areas meet to negotiate. This model is consistent with the pragmatic, business-like arrangement embodied in the *Constitution Act, 1867*. The first ministers' conference has also been used on several occasions to bargain about other parts of the constitution — even Charter rights. The problems with this process were vividly illustrated by the week-long first ministers' meeting in June 1990 on the Meech Lake Accord.

3. Problems

The absence of any means of dealing with sex equality in the *Constitution Act, 1867* corresponded with a legal system that also ignored the issue. Most of the constitutional law cases that went to court prior to the Charter involved jurisdiction. Of necessity, all issues tended to be formulated within that framework. Thus, until the Charter, even claims involving freedom of expression or racial discrimination were cast in terms of "**This level** of government can't limit my rights; only the **other** government can." This was not the ideal way to protect fundamental rights and freedoms.

The division of powers in the *Constitution Act, 1867* affected women profoundly, even though women had no say in where the lines were drawn. In fact, the lines of jurisdiction were carved across women's lives.

Family law provides a good illustration. The federal government has power over marriage and divorce. Provincial governments have power over the solemnization of marriage, and property and civil rights. It follows that the provinces can pass laws requiring support payments, allowing for the division of matrimonial property, and providing for the guardianship, custody, adoption, and legitimacy of children. But the federal government, in the *Divorce Act*, also allows for support payments and for orders regarding child custody and access. The *Divorce Act* does not allow for orders dividing matrimonial property. And although the provinces can pass legislation regulating how marriages are celebrated, they cannot pass legislation regulating how marriages are ended.

Divided jurisdiction in matters of family law means that women often are shunted from court to court, or even province to province, as they attempt to obtain and enforce court orders for the division of property, custody, and support for themselves and their children. When a change in circumstances requires a woman to return to court to have an order altered, a whole new set of jurisdictional issues can arise. Clearly, neither the division of powers nor the relevant judicial institutions were developed with the welfare of families in mind. Structures that would suit the legal needs of government and commerce were the goal of the Fathers of Confederation. The possibility of family law disputes such as we see today, for example, over matrimonial property or custody of children, would never have crossed their minds. Why would it, when divorce was granted very rarely, when a woman had no claim to any property in her husband's name, and men had the near-absolute right to guardianship of their children? Only in recent years have serious attempts been made to deal with this problem by creating unified family courts in some provinces.

A second example is social programs. Because of the division of powers, provincial governments have legislative authority over matters such as pensions, disability benefits, funding for child care, battered women's shelters, and most other social programs. Yet the federal government has the upper hand when it comes to taxation. This means that the development and funding of national social programs is a long and difficult process. The federal government raises the money through taxation and transfers it to the provinces for use in social assistance, medical care, or education. Because these are areas of exclusive provincial jurisdiction, the provinces resist any strings being attached to the funds provided. In turn, the federal government is unhappy about provincial governments simply taking the money and using it for building highways, sports stadiums, or whatever else they wish.

Amending the Constitution

1. Before 1982

Prior to 1982, most[37] amendments to the Canadian constitution could be made only through legislation passed by the Parliament of the United Kingdom. There was a convention that the British Parliament would pass the legislation upon request, but no certainty that it would do so (especially no certainty that it would do so at the sole request of the federal government). After the *Patriation Reference* case was decided by the Supreme Court of Canada, it became clear that there was a convention (but not a legal requirement) that amendments be made only at the **joint** request of the federal government and a substantial number of the provinces.[38] The amending procedure was changed through the passage of the *Canada Act, 1982* by the Parliament of the United Kingdom.

2. The current situation

The *Constitution Act, 1982* now provides for five different amending procedures as follows:

(a) Section 38 provides a general amending formula, requiring resolutions of the federal Parliament plus the legislatures of two-thirds of the provinces representing 50 per cent of the population of the provinces. The population requirement means either Ontario or Quebec must agree. The numbers requirement means that nothing could be pushed through without the agreement of at least one Western province and one Atlantic province (two-thirds means seven provinces at present). This formula applies to all situations not otherwise specified (thus, for example, it governs amendments to the *Canadian Charter of Rights and Freedoms*) and to a list of matters specified in section 42, including:

   (i) the proportion of representation by province in the House of Commons;

   (ii) powers of the Senate, method of selecting senators, and number of senators from each province;

   (iii) the Supreme Court of Canada (except for its composition, which can be changed only with unanimous agreement);[39]

   (iv) the establishment of new provinces and the extension of existing provinces into the territories.

Section 39 provides a three-year deadline for the required number of assents to be obtained. If they are obtained, the Governor General may proclaim the amendment[40] and it will take effect.[41] (However, the operation of the deadlines is ambiguous; this became apparent in the closing hours of the Meech Lake Accord.)

(b) Section 41 specifies that all legislatures (federal and provincial) must agree to constitutional amendments regarding:

   (i) the office of the Queen, the Governor General, and the Lieutenant Governors of provinces;

   (ii) the number of members from a province in the House of Commons;[42]

   (iii) certain amendments relating to the use of English or French;

   (iv) the composition of the Supreme Court of Canada;[43]

   (v) an amendment to the amending procedures.

(c) Section 43 provides a procedure for amendments that affect some but not all provinces (such as an alteration to boundaries between certain provinces). In such cases, Parliament and the legislatures of the provinces affected must agree.

(d) Section 44 provides a procedure for amendments to the executive government of Canada or the Senate and House of Commons (except for those issues affecting provincial rights, where section 41 or 42 applies). Where section 44 applies, Parliament alone may pass constitutional amendments.

(e) Section 45 allows for provincial legislatures to amend their own provincial constitutions, except where the amendment relates to the office of the Lieutenant Governor.[44]

Compared with constitutions of other federal states, our constitution is unusual in its unanimity requirements.[45] The presence of these requirements is explained largely by history rather than by rational considerations.[46] As shown by the demise of the Meech Lake Accord, unanimity makes constitutional amendment very difficult to achieve.

Canadian Charter of Rights and Freedoms

1. Overall structure of the Charter

The *Canadian Charter of Rights and Freedoms* is part of the *Constitution Act, 1982*. Most parts of the Charter came into effect on April 17, 1982. (The exception was the equality rights provision, section 15, which was delayed until April 17, 1985.) Prior to the Charter, there was no real guarantee that governments would not infringe fundamental rights and freedoms (such as freedom of speech, freedom of religion, or equality before the law). The *Canadian Bill of Rights*, which came into effect in 1960 and deals with some of these rights and freedoms, is simply a federal statute like any other, and its wording is generally much more limited than that of the Charter. The *Bill of Rights* applies only to the federal government, while the Charter applies to both federal and provincial governments (and, most likely, to subsidiary forms of government such as municipalities).

As part of the constitution, the Charter is "entrenched", meaning it can't be changed or amended without constitutional amendment.[47] Thus, changes to the Charter cannot be made easily or unilaterally by any province or the federal government. The Charter is part of "the supreme law of Canada", and legislation that violates Charter rights is therefore invalid. The Supreme Court of Canada stated these general principles in one of its early decisions about the Charter:

> *The Constitution of a country is a statement of the will of the people to be governed in accordance with certain principles held as fundamental and certain prescriptions restrictive of the powers of the legislature and government. It is, as s. 52 of the Constitution Act, 1982 declares, the "supreme law" of the nation, unalterable by the normal legislative process, and unsuffering of laws inconsistent with it. The duty of the judiciary is to interpret and apply the laws of Canada and each of the provinces, and it is thus our duty to ensure that the constitutional law prevails.*[48]

Section 1 guarantees and limitations

The Canadian Charter of Rights and Freedoms guarantees the rights and freedoms set out in it subject only to such reasonable limits prescribed by law as can be demonstrably justified in a free and democratic society.

Section 1 serves two important functions. First, it guarantees the rights and freedoms defined in other sections of the Charter. Second, it permits governments to infringe those rights in some circumstances.[49]

A recent example of the operation of section 1 is the Supreme Court decision on soliciting. Section 213(1)(c) of the *Criminal Code* says that a person is guilty of a criminal offence if, in a public place or any place open to public view, he or she "in any manner communicates or attempts to communicate with any person for the purpose of engaging in prostitution or of obtaining the sexual services of a prostitute..." . The majority of the Court held that the law was inconsistent with section 2(b) of the Charter, which protects the right to freedom of expression. But the Court also said that even though the law was inconsistent with the Charter, it was justifiable because Parliament was implementing the important government objective of trying to eliminate the social nuisance created by street solicitation. Moreover, the majority said, the right to communicate about exchanging sex for money is not a centrally important one. Madam Justice Wilson and Madam Justice L'Heureux-Dubé, the two women who sat on the case, disagreed. They said that the law was **not** justifiable as required by section 1:

> ... communicating or attempting to communicate with someone in a public place with respect to the sale of sexual services does not automatically create a nuisance any more than communicating or attempting to communicate with someone on the sidewalk to promote a candidate for municipal election. Moreover, as already mentioned, prostitution is itself a perfectly legal activity and the avowed objective of the legislature was not to make it illegal but only, as the Minister of Justice emphasized at the time, to deal with the nuisance created by street solicitation. It seems to me that to render criminal the communicative acts of persons engaged in a lawful activity which is not shown to be harming anybody cannot be justified by the legislative objective advanced in its support.[50]

This example shows that a judge must first decide whether a law violates the Charter. If it does, the judge must then decide whether the law serves to benefit society generally to such an extent that it justifies violating the individual rights in question. It also shows that there are no simple answers about whether Charter violations are permitted under section 1 — the judges in the soliciting case came to different conclusions, even though they were applying the same law.

Although not all feminists agree on the issue of prostitution, most would be uncomfortable with the outcome of this case because leaving the law against soliciting in place probably increases the risk of harm to women who work as street prostitutes. Such a law gives them a strong incentive to stay out of sight of police, thereby putting them at greater risk of attack. The Court decided in an earlier case[51] that communications in pursuit of commercial gain are protected by the freedom of speech guarantee. In putting society's need to protect itself against nuisance ahead of the right of prostitutes to free speech, the Court gave low priority to the physical safety of a group that is mostly female. Yet this case also illustrates the limits on what a court can do. A decision favouring the right of prostitutes to freedom of expression would not necessarily have led to any improvement in their lives.

Women's organizations and others were concerned about including section 1 in the Charter, because it gives the courts room to permit violations of Charter rights. However, section 1 also permits courts to uphold laws that benefit women, even when the laws come under attack because they violate someone else's individual rights. An example of this is the *Criminal Code* prohibition against publishing the names of sexual assault victims.[52] This law was upheld under section 1. Former Chief Justice Dickson has said that the courts must avoid letting the Charter be used to roll back legislative gains made by disadvantaged groups in society, and section 1 provides the mechanism which may be used to prevent such outcomes.[53]

Section 1 highlights the new role conferred on the judiciary by the Charter, which requires courts to define fundamental rights, determine whether they have been violated, then balance the significance of the violation against the interests of society as a whole. Despite the courts' attempts to create a clear and predictable way of achieving this balance, it is evident that the result may depend on the social and political views of the judge who hears a case. This emphasizes the importance of the judicial appointment process and judicial education programs.[54]

Section 33 — The vulnerability of the Charter

Parliament or the legislature of a province may expressly declare in an Act of Parliament or of the legislature, as the case may be, that the Act or a provision thereof shall operate notwithstanding a provision included in section 2 or sections 7 to 15 of this Charter.

This means Parliament or any provincial legislature can pass legislation regardless of the Charter. Section 33 is sometimes called the "override" or the "notwithstanding" clause. Because of it, many important elements in the Charter are not fully protected: they are not truly entrenched. Only a few of the rights and freedoms named in the Charter are **not** subject to section 33 and cannot be overridden by Parliament or a legislature: democratic rights, mobility rights, language rights, and section 28 (guaranteeing that everything in the Charter applies equally to male and female persons). However, most of the rights and freedoms discussed here **are vulnerable** to the override, including:

- the fundamental freedoms (religion, expression, assembly, association);
- the legal rights (the right to life, liberty and security of the person, the right to be free from unreasonable search or seizure); and
- the equality rights in section 15.

The only restriction on the use of the section 33 override is that there is a "sunset clause", which means that each use of it expires automatically after five years. The section 33 override clause has been used by only two governments to date (Saskatchewan and Quebec).[55]

Section 33 is controversial because it detracts from the absolute protection of Charter rights. Many argue, however, that it is consistent with responsible government, giving the final word in many cases to elected legislatures rather than to judges. The existence of sections 1 and 33 makes Canada's constitution very different from that of the United States, which contains no such provisions.

The interpretive sections 28, 27, 25

Three sections of the Charter give direction to the courts about how to interpret its rights and freedoms:

> 28. *Notwithstanding anything in this Charter, the rights and freedoms referred to in it are guaranteed equally to male and female persons.*
>
> 27. *This Charter shall be interpreted in a manner consistent with the preservation and enhancement of the multicultural heritage of Canadians.*
>
> 25. *The guarantee in this Charter of certain rights and freedoms shall not be construed so as to abrogate or derogate from any aboriginal, treaty or other rights or freedoms that pertain to the aboriginal peoples of Canada including*
>
>   (a) *any rights or freedoms that have been recognized by the Royal Proclamation of October 7, 1763; and*
>
>   (b) *any rights or freedoms that now exist by way of land claims agreements or may be so acquired.*

Section 28, of course, is of particular importance to women. The most strongly worded of the interpretive clauses, it states that equality between the sexes is of paramount importance. It prevents the use of the section 33 override where legislation denies a Charter right or freedom to women (or men). Although section 28 has not been referred to frequently in Charter cases, its presence may well have made a difference to the courts' approach to sex equality cases and to issues such as reproductive choice.[56] The failure to mention section 28 in one part of the Meech Lake Accord was one of the major concerns of the women's organizations that sought changes to the Accord.[57]

Sections 27 and 25 are naturally important to the women directly affected by them (as members of multicultural communities or First Nations peoples). But they are also important to women in Canada generally because they show respect for diversity, a necessary element in women's claims to equality.

The enforcement sections 24 and 52

The fact that rights are listed in the Charter does not mean that they are reflected in reality. In most cases, it is necessary to take steps to enforce them. These steps can be in the political arena, pointing out to government that changes in law, policy, or administrative practice are necessary to comply with the Charter. In that context, section 52 of the *Constitution Act, 1982* states:

> 52. (1) *The Constitution of Canada is the supreme law of Canada, and any law that is inconsistent with the provisions of the Constitution is, to the extent of the inconsistency, of no force or effect.*

Governments should therefore be motivated to change laws that are inconsistent with the provisions of the constitution. This motivation is not always present, however, and there is often disagreement about whether laws or practices are consistent with the Charter. In these situations, steps can be taken through the court system.

Section 24(1) of the Charter says:
Anyone whose rights or freedoms, as guaranteed by this Charter, have been infringed or denied may apply to a court of competent jurisdiction to obtain such remedy as the court considers appropriate and just in the circumstances.

This means that courts can make orders to give effect to Charter rights, after hearing evidence and argument. But that occurs only if the case actually gets to court and is heard. In fact, raising issues through litigation is often difficult, if not impossible. The expense and energy involved in presenting a court case are always considerable and sometimes staggering. Although limited financial assistance is available for some types of cases, and advocacy groups can help with certain kinds of claims, the litigation process is usually beyond the resources of ordinary people.[58] For that reason, and because litigation is not always the ideal way to bring about change, other alternatives should always be considered first.

With this structure of the Charter in mind, and these limits on its rights and freedoms understood, we turn now to the actual contents of the Charter and the rights and freedoms it guarantees.

2. Contents of the Charter

The rights and freedoms guaranteed in the Charter fall into four categories: liberty rights and freedoms, legal rights, twentieth century rights, and the Canadian clauses.[59]

(a) Liberty rights and freedoms
(i) Fundamental freedoms

Section 2 of the Charter is labelled "fundamental freedoms". It guarantees the traditional "civil liberties" found in all written bills of rights. They are an expression of the long struggle for individual freedom in western society. Section 2 reads:

Everyone has the following fundamental freedoms:
- *freedom of conscience and religion;*
- *freedom of thought, belief, opinion and expression, including freedom of the press and other media of communication;*
- *freedom of peaceful assembly; and*
- *freedom of association.*

The exercise of these freedoms is guaranteed to women as well as men (beyond doubt, by virtue of section 28). In some ways, the fundamental freedoms guaranteed in section 2 support women's equality. For example, Madam Justice Bertha Wilson of the Supreme Court of Canada based her decision in the *Morgentaler* case on the "freedom of conscience and religion" clause. The same section prevents the establishment of an official state religion in Canada.[60]

Freedom of assembly and of association protect women's rights to organize in groups, to hold demonstrations, and so on. However, in the context of trade union activity, freedom of association has been interpreted restrictively by the majority of the Supreme Court of Canada.[61] The courts' treatment of challenges to single-sex organizations will be important for women.[62]

The guarantee of freedom of thought, belief, opinion, and expression is a double-edged sword. While guaranteeing women's right to hold views and express them, section 2(b) does not guarantee that women will have access to media of communication so that those views can be made known. At the same time, section 2(b) empowers those few who do have access to media to express their views. In the *Keegstra* case, the Supreme Court of Canada found that the laws making it a crime to promote hatred against minority groups such as Jews constituted a violation of freedom of expression, but upheld them under section 1. The Court noted that the laws were very narrowly drafted and that they served the purpose of promoting equality as guaranteed under section 15 of the Charter, as well as multiculturalism contemplated under section 27.[63] The Court has not yet decided a case involving the constitutionality of criminal laws about pornography.[64]

Freedom of expression can conflict with women's rights in another type of situation: the protection of sexual assault survivors from having their names reported during trials against their alleged attackers. The Supreme Court of Canada upheld the *Criminal Code* protection of survivors, despite a claim by a newspaper chain that its freedom of expression was infringed.[65]

(ii) Democratic rights

The democratic rights in sections 3 to 5 of the Charter mesh with the civil liberties in section 2. Section 3 says:

Every citizen of Canada has the right to vote in an election of members of the House of Commons or of a legislative assembly and to be qualified for membership therein.

Women achieved the right to vote and recognition as persons only in this century. The combined effect of section 3 and section 28 (neither of which is subject to the section 33 override) means that, short of a constitutional amendment, a legislature can never deprive women of the right to vote.[66]

The courts have interpreted section 3 to mean that it must be reasonably possible for votes to be cast[67] and there must be some reasonable approximation of "one person, one vote". The Supreme Court of Canada has held, however, that the central purpose of section 3 is not to guarantee "representation by population", but **effective** representation.[68]

While the basic right to vote is a necessary condition for political participation, it does not guarantee meaningful representation. Further, it has done nothing to ensure even minimal participation by women in constitutional change. There may be methods of election that would achieve better representation than our existing one. The argument that representative democracy is not necessarily the ideal democratic system must also be considered. (These points are elaborated on below.)

(iii) Life, liberty, and security of the person

Although section 7 of the Charter is found under the label "legal rights", in some important ways it belongs with civil liberties. It reads:

Everyone has the right to life, liberty and security of the person and the right not to be deprived thereof except in accordance with the principles of fundamental justice.

Section 7 does not guarantee the right to life, liberty, and security of the person in all circumstances. What it guarantees is that people will not be deprived of these rights except in accordance with the principles of fundamental justice. Thus, if the principles of fundamental justice are observed, there can be laws under which people are imprisoned, subjected to searches, or perhaps even executed. But section 7 does guarantee that where life, liberty, and security of the person are affected by laws or government activities, the law or activity can be reviewed to see whether it is in accordance with the principles of fundamental justice.

The courts have said that legislation violates section 7 if it permits deprivation of life, liberty, or security of the person without procedural fairness. For example, the old *Immigration Act* procedures for assessing refugee claims, which didn't allow for a hearing, were struck down in the *Singh* case.[69] As well, legislation that is simply inconsistent with basic principles of our legal system may also violate section 7. The provincial law whereby people could go to jail if they drove motor vehicles while their licences were suspended, even if they didn't know about the suspension, was held unconstitutional for that reason.[70]

Who is entitled to the protection of section 7? The Supreme Court of Canada has said that a corporation is not.[71] And, crucially for women, the Court has not yet finally determined whether "everyone" includes a fetus.[72] Although the **constitutional** status of the fetus has not been explicitly decided by the Supreme Court, the Court made it very clear in *Daigle v. Tremblay* and in *R. v. Sullivan and Lemay*[73] that, unless a legislature explicitly states otherwise (and maybe not even then), a fetus is not a "person" in either Anglo-Canadian common law or Quebec civil law,[74] under the *Criminal Code* of Canada.

The meaning of the terms "life, liberty and security of the person" is being developed by the courts. "Liberty" has been held by some courts to extend beyond physical liberty to matters such as the right to practise a profession.[75] On the other hand, the courts have also indicated that section 7 does not extend to property and economic rights.[76] The potential of section 7 to protect "social rights", such as a right to food, shelter, or health care, has not yet been explored. One of the major stumbling blocks to success for such claims would be that they would entail ordering governments to set up programs and pay for them — not the sort of orders that courts are accustomed to issuing, or governments to obeying.

In the *Morgentaler* case, Madam Justice Bertha Wilson discussed "liberty". She said:
Thus, an aspect of the respect for human dignity on which the Charter is founded is the right to make fundamental personal decisions without interference from the state. This right is a critical component of the right to liberty.[77]

About a woman's decision to have an abortion, Justice Wilson wrote:
It is not just a medical decision; it is a profound social and ethical one as well. [A woman's] response to it will be the response of the whole person. . . . It is probably impossible for a man to respond, even imaginatively, to such a dilemma not just because it is outside the realm of his personal experience . . . but because he can relate to it only by objectifying it, thereby eliminating the subjective elements of the female psyche which are at the heart of the dilemma.[78]

Justice Wilson noted that the history of human rights has been a chronicle of men struggling against an overbearing state apparatus. The goal of the struggle for women's rights has been to put women in the same position as men:
Thus, women's needs and aspirations are only now being translated into protected rights. The right to reproduce or not to reproduce which is in issue in this case is one such right and is properly perceived as an integral part of modern woman's struggle to assert her dignity and worth as a human being.[79]

However, it was under the right to "security of the person", rather than "liberty", that the majority of the Court struck down the old abortion law (section 251 of the *Criminal Code*) in the *Morgentaler* case.[80]

(b) Legal rights

Legal rights refer to the individual's protection against the exercise of state power, whether through police, government administrators, or the courts. Legal rights fall into three categories: basic underlying protections, specifically criminal law rights, and rights pertaining to witnesses.

(i) Basic underlying protections (sections 7, 8, 9, 10, and 12)

We discussed section 7 in connection with "fundamental freedoms". It states the basic principle underlying all the legal rights: if the state is going to interfere with an individual's life, liberty, or security of the person it must justify its actions. Section 7 states a general right; the other legal rights in sections 8 to 14 are specific instances of this general right.

Section 8 says:
Everyone has the right to be secure against unreasonable search or seizure.

This protects against laws or activities (whether by the police or others) relating to searches of people or property, and seizure of objects. The Supreme Court of Canada has said that section 8 protects an individual's reasonable expectations of privacy.[81]

Like some other Charter rights, a right to privacy could work for or against women. While constitutional protection for the right to abortion in the United States was based on the right to privacy, recent court decisions there have shown that this was a shaky foundation.[82] Arguments about privacy rights also have the potential to enforce domestic isolation and vulnerability to abuse as in the view that wife battering is a "private" or "domestic" matter.

Sections 9 and 12 also limit the scope of state power to detain or imprison people and to inflict cruel or unusual punishment.[83]

Section 10 confers rights on those who have been arrested or detained, whether by police, customs officers, or others acting under authority of law.[84]

(ii) Specifically criminal law rights (section 11)

The rights protected by section 11[85] — the right to be tried within a reasonable time and the right to a fair and public hearing before an independent and impartial tribunal — have provided the basis for claims that clash with some feminist objectives.[86] For example, in the *Seaboyer* case decided in 1991, the Supreme Court of Canada held that the right to a fair trial under s. 11(d) was violated by the *Criminal Code* rules which prohibited evidence about the previous sexual conduct of the complainant.[87] Those rules, though not perfect, were the outcome of a long and hard battle by women's organizations to achieve such protection.

(iii) Rights pertaining to witnesses (sections 13 and 14)

Section 13 applies to anyone who is a witness in any proceeding, either criminal or civil. It reads:

> *A witness who testifies in any proceedings has the right not to have any incriminating evidence so given used to incriminate that witness in any other proceedings, except in a prosecution for perjury or for the giving of contradictory evidence.*

This is the Canadian version of the U.S. Fifth Amendment. The difference is that under Canadian law a witness may not **refuse** to answer a question on the ground that the answer she gives might tend to incriminate her. Instead, she is compelled to answer such questions (and if she refuses she is liable to criminal punishment), but she is protected by section 13 of the Charter from having those answers used against her in later proceedings.[88] In many instances (although not all) a spouse is treated like any other witness, that is, she can be forced to testify against her spouse.[89]

Section 14 is important for women with impaired hearing and for women who do not speak the language in which proceedings are being conducted. It says:

> *A party or witness in any proceedings who does not understand or speak the language in which the proceedings are conducted or who is deaf has the right to the assistance of an interpreter.*

Although providing interpreters has been the practice in most jurisdictions for some time, having it enshrined as a constitutional right is important. The wording of the section makes it clear that it applies in all proceedings, including criminal trials, civil trials, and hearings before other tribunals such as labour arbitration boards.

(c) Twentieth-century rights

This expression refers to rights that have come to be recognized only in this century, not just in Canada, but also in other parts of the world. The equality rights in sections 15 and 28 and the group interests recognized in sections 25 and 27 are of this nature.

(i) Equality rights

The equality rights section reads as follows:

> 15. (1) *Every individual is equal before and under the law and has the right to the equal protection and equal benefit of the law without discrimination and, in particular, without discrimination based on race, national or ethnic origin, colour, religion, sex, age or mental or physical disability.*
>
> (2) *Subsection (1) does not preclude any law, program or activity that has as its object the amelioration of conditions of disadvantaged individuals or groups including those that are disadvantaged because of race, national or ethnic origin, colour, religion, sex, age or mental or physical disability.*

When the Charter was being drafted, sections 15 and 28 were of crucial interest to women. Though hardly perfect, sections 15 and 28 have the potential to provide a stronger constitutional foundation for equality claims than exists in most parts of the world.[90] Not many section 15 cases dealing with women's equality have been argued. Even so, given the recent Supreme Court decisions that have referred to section 15 and to human rights legislation, there is still good reason for optimism.[91] In addition, because the Charter is seen as reflecting the values of the nation, strong equality provisions have an important effect in setting the tone for policy and decision-making.

In 1989, the Canadian Advisory Council on the Status of Women published *Canadian Charter Equality Rights for Women: One Step Forward or Two Steps Back?* by Gwen Brodsky and Shelagh Day.[92] The book contains an extensive review of the equality cases that came before the courts in the first three years that section 15 was in effect. It also describes some theoretical approaches to equality. To avoid duplicating that material, our discussion of equality rights will be brief.

One of the major concerns about section 15 was that although it was meant to eliminate the disadvantages suffered by groups discriminated against historically, it could be used for completely different purposes.[93] For example, many of the initial cases under section 15 involved claims that governmental regulation of business created unconstitutional inequalities. Zoning by-laws, for instance, placed different restrictions on what can be built in different parts of a city. There was a real risk that the meaning of "equality" in section 15 would become distorted if developed through cases such as this.

In its first three section 15 cases, the Supreme Court ruled out such claims.[94] It said that section 15 cases must relate to enumerated or analogous grounds (meaning the grounds enumerated or listed in section 15— race, religion, sex, and so on or grounds similar to them). The Court emphasized that the common thread running through the enumerated grounds was that they referred to historically disadvantaged groups, including groups that could be described as "discrete and insular minorities". The Court said the decision about whether a group is protected under section 15 should be made "in the context of the place of the group in the entire social, political and legal fabric of our society."[95] Thus, for example, the Court could make a comparison between discrimination based on sexual orientation and discrimination based on the grounds listed in section 15, find that sexual orientation counts as an analogous ground under section 15, and conclude that a given law or government activity is unconstitutional and invalid.

"Discrimination" was defined in these cases using principles developed under human rights law.[96] Carrying over this definition should mean that, under section 15 of the Charter, both intentional and unintentional discrimination are prohibited. Designing a university building so that there are no elevators in the wing housing faculty offices might not be intended to keep students in wheelchairs from visiting members of faculty, but it certainly has that effect. The courts have ruled that this kind of unintentional discrimination is prohibited by human rights legislation.

It should also mean that principles developed in human rights cases such as *Brooks v. Canada Safeway*[97] (the case about pregnant women being excluded from disability insurance plans) will be carried over into Charter cases. Pregnant women who are disadvantaged by legislation would have a good argument that their Charter rights have been violated. *Brooks* also paves the way for an argument that abortion is an equality issue (and thus, for example, that a provincial law restricting public funding for abortions under the medical insurance scheme is unconstitutional). Finally, in *Brooks* the Supreme Court of Canada recognized the value of childbearing in a concrete way, which confers new benefits on pregnant women. Since childbearing and childrearing have always been women's work — unpaid and often unacknowledged — this is a heartening and dramatic change.

In a second human rights case decided at the same time as *Brooks*, the Supreme Court of Canada found that human rights legislation prohibiting sex discrimination provides protection against sexual harassment. An employer is obliged to provide a harassment-free workplace. And the Court took into account the effects of a power imbalance on women employees, saying:

> *When sexual harassment occurs in the workplace, it is an abuse of both economic and sexual power. Sexual harassment is a demeaning practice, one that constitutes a profound affront to the dignity of the employees forced to endure it. By requiring an employee to contend with unwelcome · sexual actions or explicit sexual demands, sexual harassment in the workplace attacks the dignity and self-respect of the victim both as an employee and as a human being.*[98]

This approach to equality is another encouraging sign for women about the potential of section 15.

Section 15(2), which permits affirmative action programs, should eliminate much of the debate that has surrounded such programs in the United States. The very fact that such programs are contemplated in the definition of rights under section 15 underlines the meaning of those rights. These programs are designed to eliminate comparative disadvantage, rather than continue it by treating everyone alike, whatever their circumstances.

(d) The Canadian clauses

The "Canadian clauses" refer to the parts of the Charter that address uniquely Canadian concerns and reflect political compromises. They determine the relationship between groups of Canadians, as defined by language, by Aboriginal status, by religion, by ethnic background, or by economic region of the country. Unlike Charter rights aimed at protecting individuals against the state, these are "collective rights" aimed at preserving or enhancing the position of groups of people.

The provisions for the official languages of Canada are in sections 16 to 22. They state that Canada and New Brunswick have French and English as their official languages. The other nine provinces have not chosen to be officially bilingual; but they could be included in these sections through a constitutional amendment requiring resolutions of the provinces affected, the Senate, and the House of Commons.[99]

Minority language educational rights (in section 23) give the right to have one's children receive primary and secondary school instruction in a minority language (English or French) in certain circumstances.[100]

The constitution contains two provisions regarding Aboriginal people: one in Section 25 of the Charter (set out above), the other in the *Constitution Act, 1982*. Section 35 of the *Constitution Act, 1982* states:

(1) The existing aboriginal and treaty rights of the aboriginal peoples of Canada are hereby recognized and affirmed.

(2) In this Act, "aboriginal peoples of Canada" includes the Indian, Inuit and Métis peoples of Canada.

(3) For greater certainty, in subsection (1) "treaty rights" includes rights that now exist by way of land claims agreements or may be so acquired.

(4) Notwithstanding any other provision of this Act, the aboriginal and treaty rights referred to in subsection (1) are guaranteed equally to male and female persons.

One of the main reasons for adding section 35(4) in 1983 was long-standing discrimination against Indian women under the *Indian Act*. Formerly, when Indian women married non-Indian men, they lost Indian status and so did their children. However, when an Indian man married a non-Indian woman, he not only retained his status but conferred it on his wife and children. These rules reflected Victorian patriarchal norms more than they did the kinship practices of First Nations people. Yet this blatantly unfair system was upheld in 1974 by the Supreme Court of

Canada in a challenge under the *Canadian Bill of Rights*.[101] Despite a successful complaint to the United Nations Human Rights Committee (on the basis that a member of a cultural minority has the right to associate with other members of her cultural group),[102] no legislative change occurred. Finally in 1985, the *Indian Act* was amended[103] in a way that restored equality only partially: women who lost status by marriage can regain their status, but band membership and entitlement to share in band resources do not automatically follow. Further, the children of women who lost Indian status do not gain status, even though the children of Indian men and non-Indian women keep their status.

Section 29 protects pre-existing constitutional arrangements regarding denominational schools, such as the Ontario government's funding of Roman Catholic schools.[104]

Canada's ethnic and cultural composition is addressed in section 27:
This Charter shall be interpreted in a manner consistent with the preservation and enhancement of the multicultural heritage of Canadians.

This section is important where legislation might help or hurt multicultural interests. For example, the criminal law against promoting hatred can further multicultural interests.[105] On the other hand, Sunday closing laws, which assume that Sunday is everyone's day of rest, can hinder such interests.[106]

Finally, the mobility rights set out in section 6 state that every Canadian citizen has "the right to enter, remain in and leave Canada", and that every Canadian citizen and permanent resident has the right to live and work in any province. The only limit on this is that there are residency requirements for social services. This restricts the mobility of people (predominantly women and children) who depend on these services.

Provinces trying to make their living conditions more attractive have scope to do so. Section 6(4) preserves the right of governments to pass laws or create programs to improve "conditions of individuals in that province who are socially or economically disadvantaged" where the employment rate in the province is below the national rate.

(e) Omissions from the Charter

Certain issues are not dealt with in the Charter. For example, the right to property is not mentioned, although it is in the *Canadian Bill of Rights*. Although entrenching property rights in the constitution has been discussed from time to time, this has not been done. One explanation is that it is simply unnecessary. The common law developed over hundreds of years has been concerned largely with regulating and preserving property rights. Further, although in many cases courts have said that the Charter does not provide a right to property, they have decided cases in ways that have that effect. For example, in one of the first cases decided by the Supreme Court on the Charter, it protected a large newspaper chain from searches under the *Combines Investigation*

Act.[107] In the leading case on mobility rights, the Supreme Court struck down a law that interfered with the ability of lawyers to work in national law firms.[108]

Generally, entrenching property rights would work against women, simply because women own less property. A constitutional property right might undermine provincial laws that provide for an equitable division of property upon divorce. In the majority of cases, women are the spouses who are seeking, rather than resisting, division of property. Finally, entrenching property rights could make it even more difficult to develop and maintain social programs. Again, because women are economically disadvantaged and are primarily responsible for child care and for care of elderly relatives, social programs tend to be much more important to women than to men.

The Charter also fails to provide (explicitly at least) for social rights — such as the right to nourishment, shelter, medical assistance, or education. It could be argued that various sections of the Charter do provide for social rights. Certainly, wording such as "equal benefit of the law" in section 15 and "security of the person" in section 7 might have this potential. As well, section 36 of the *Constitution Act, 1982* should not be overlooked. It states:

(1) Without altering the legislative authority of Parliament or of the provincial legislatures, or the rights of any of them with respect to the exercise of their legislative authority, Parliament and the legislatures, together with the government of Canada and the provincial governments, are committed to

(a) promoting equal opportunities for the well-being of Canadians;

(b) furthering economic development to reduce disparity in opportunities; and

(c) providing essential public services of reasonable quality to all Canadians.

(2) Parliament and the government of Canada are committed to the principle of making equalization payments to ensure that provincial governments have sufficient revenues to provide reasonably comparable levels of public services at reasonably comparable levels of taxation.

Although this section does not explicitly provide the basis for a claim by women, for example, to adequate resources for themselves and their children, it does state a principle that could be important in political or legal decisions.

Finally, Charter rights relate only to governments or law.[109] Private individuals are not held to the same standards. This means that, for example, if a private property owner refuses to rent to a single mother, this act of discrimination must be dealt with under provincial human rights legislation rather than the Charter.[110]

Discussion Questions

Part 2: What are the important principles of Canada's Constitution?

1. Identify some important principles of Canada's constitution. Should any of these be changed? Why? How? What principles would you include?

2. How well are women represented in Canada's three branches of government — legislative, executive, and judicial?

3. Do you think having more women in the legislatures, cabinet, public service, and judiciary will make a difference?

4. Identify some ways that the division of powers between the federal and provincial/territorial governments affects women. What changes would you make in this area?

5. Identify the ways in which our constitution can be amended. How do you think constitutional amendments should take place?

6. Discuss the potential of the *Canadian Charter of Rights and Freedoms* for advancing the status of women in Canada.

7. What has been left out of the Charter? What would you include?

How the Constitution Got This Way

This section will:

- Briefly review the history of women's participation in public life in Canada up to 1982, including constitution-making, focussing on the colonial constitutional tradition, restrictions on the right to vote, women's participation in formal and informal political life, and the recommendations of the Royal Commission on the Status of Women;
- briefly review women's participation in the struggle for the inclusion of equality rights in the Canadian Charter and describe continuing obstacles to women's participation in politics and constitution-making.

History Up to the Charter

The first Europeans to settle in Canada brought with them the idea of formal written constitutions. These were imposed on the Aboriginal systems already in effect in North America at the time, to regulate the exercise of power by Europeans. The settlers also brought with them the tradition of women's subordination and, specifically, women's exclusion from public decision-making. The military, the seigneurial system of feudal landlords, and the church of New France all relegated women to an ancillary status, though still one that was less constrained than that of their sisters in the old world.[1] The condition of women colonists of British descent was similar.[2] As wives or daughters, as nuns, as servants or slaves, women laboured in the fields, worked in trade, raised children, and kept the home-fires burning, no small feat in the hostile winters of their new country.[3]

The conquest of New France in 1759 and the resulting Treaty of Paris, signed in 1763, united the colonies under British rule. Under the English laws of colonization, the laws that settlers brought with them became the laws of the colonies.[4] During this era, women's political participation was limited to members of the First Nations within their own communities. A number of Aboriginal women were among those who signed treaties between their people and the British colonizers.[5]

In 1791, the colonies of Upper and Lower Canada received their first British-style constitution. Forged in the aftermath of the American War of Independence, it reflected loyalty to the monarchy and commitment to a strong central authority — the governor chosen by Britain. He in turn chose an executive council, drawn from members of a wealthy elite.[6] Provision was made for representative assemblies in Upper and Lower Canada, but these did not have much power, because their ability to levy taxes and spend money was limited.[7] The vote was given to all "persons" in Upper and Lower Canada who held a requisite amount of property.[8]

Although it seems to have been assumed generally that women did not qualify to vote, the legislature of New Brunswick found it necessary to make this explicit.[9] Women in the other colonies took advantage of the ambiguity and cast their votes.[10] Although it was not widespread, this practice eventually became controversial, and in 1832 the Assembly of Lower Canada passed a measure prohibiting women from voting. The British government passed similar legislation the same year,[11] and when Upper and Lower Canada united, that legislature followed suit in 1849.[12] A number of reasons were put forward for denying women the vote, among them, their susceptibility to influence by fathers or husbands and the perils of the rowdy political process.[13]

Despite being formally barred from the electoral process, some women were able to have an indirect influence. Wives or mistresses of powerful men, and women working in education, industry, medicine or religious orders, were politically active in a circumscribed way.[14] First Nations women played important roles in the fur trade[15] and in other industries, as well as in their own communities. Women were active in the underground railway for escaped U.S. slaves, in the rebellion of 1837-38, and in a variety of local matters.[16] For example, they organized charitable and religious associations to deal with urban crime and poverty. In the 1850s, three groups of women petitioned the legislature of Canada West (Upper Canada/Ontario), asking for the right of married women to hold property in their own names. By 1859, they were successful. A new law was passed in Canada without British precedent.[17] This incident appears to have been isolated, however. Women did not begin to call persistently for changes in their political and legal status until somewhat later.

The first draft of the *British North America Act* was cobbled together by delegates from Canada, Newfoundland, Nova Scotia, Prince Edward Island, and New Brunswick at a meeting in Quebec in 1864. Although the deal was rejected in a general election in New Brunswick and never submitted to the legislature of Nova Scotia, delegates from four provinces (Canada West, Canada East, Nova Scotia, and New Brunswick) ultimately participated in the final version, which was passed by the British Parliament in 1867.[18] Later, the other six provinces joined Confederation, beginning with Manitoba in 1870 and most recently with Newfoundland in 1949.

Women were not present at the bargaining table from which the *British North America Act* emerged. Nor was there a counterpart to Abigail Adams, who wrote in 1776 to her husband, John Adams, to argue for just treatment of women in the laws of the new American republic. She advised him:

> *In the new code of laws which I suppose it will be necessary for you to make, I desire you would remember the ladies and be more generous and favorable to them than your ancestors. Do not put such unlimited power into the hands of the husbands. Remember, all men would be tyrants if they could. If particular care and attention is not paid to the ladies, we are determined to foment a rebellion, and will not hold ourselves bound by any laws in which we have no voice or representation.*[19]

Alas, her advice was ignored; eventually, the fomenting of rebellion was necessary. If there were any Mothers of Confederation — even in the shadows — they are absent from the official record. The "pilot of Confederation",[20] Sir John A. Macdonald, was a widower during the period in which the new constitution took shape. A painting of Queen Victoria provides the only female presence in the depiction of the final negotiations in London in 1866.

Women's concerns were not only ignored in the making of the constitution, women were also excluded specifically from the political development of the new Dominion of Canada. They were barred from voting and discouraged from public speaking. Not long after Confederation, women began to campaign actively for suffrage — the right to vote.

Women property holders in British Columbia were the first to be granted the right to vote, in 1873, but only in municipal elections — and when three women went to exercise this right, they were greeted with jibes and catcalls.[21] This serves as a reminder that a legal right does not necessarily mean an actual right. There are many unofficial obstacles to political participation.

Still, acquiring the legal right is a necessary first step. But the legal climate in which the suffragist campaign took place is captured in the comments of a U.S. judge, quoted by Mr. Justice Barker of the Supreme Court of New Brunswick. This was in 1905 when the court refused to allow a woman, Mabel Penery French, to practise law:

> *... the civil law, as well as nature herself, has always recognized a wide difference in the respective spheres and destinies of man and woman. Man is, or should be, woman's protector and defender. The natural and proper timidity and delicacy which belongs to the female sex evidently unfits it for many of the occupations of civil life. ... The paramount destiny and mission of women are to fulfil the noble and benign offices of wife and mother. This is the law of the Creator. And the rules of civil society must be adapted to the general constitution of things, and cannot be based upon exceptional cases.*[22]

Struggling against the "general constitution of things", women continued to demand the vote on many fronts. Each provincial legislature and the federal Parliament had to be persuaded individually. Between 1916 and 1918 there were successes in Manitoba, Saskatchewan, British Columbia, Ontario, and Nova Scotia. In 1917, women over the age of 21 who were British subjects, and who had a close family member in the Canadian or British armed forces, were given the vote by a Conservative government seeking support for its pro-conscription stand.[23] Re-elected, the Borden government extended the franchise to women (on the same basis as men) the following year. In 1920, women won the right to hold political office and sit in Parliament.[24] However, Canadian women of Chinese, Japanese, and East Indian parentage did not achieve full suffrage until after World War II, and women with Indian status were not enfranchised federally until 1960.[25]

This did not end the legislative blockade against women's political participation. Several provinces continued to bar women from voting. Quebec was the last to concede the right, holding out until 1940.[26] Newfoundland limited the franchise to women over the age of 25 until 1946.[27]

Many other obstacles had to be overcome. Even "gender-neutral" language did not necessarily include women. For example, requests that women be appointed to the Senate were met with the excuse that women were precluded from this position by the *British North America Act*, which specified that senators must be "qualified persons". It took the *Persons Case* to settle the matter.

Tangible and intangible barriers continued to impede women's participation in Canadian political life. Before they got the vote, most women had chosen to stay out of the established political parties because they were corrupt or at best indifferent to women's interests.[28] Once suffrage was achieved, some women did become involved in partisan politics and one, Agnes Macphail, was elected to the House of Commons in 1921. Again, the political victory didn't automatically lead to equality. Here Macphail describes her first years in office:

Some members resented my intrusion, others jeered at me, while a very few were genuinely glad to see a woman in the House. Most of the members made me painfully conscious of my sex...[29]

Agnes Macphail sat as a member until 1940 and as the **only** woman member until 1935.[30]

In the 50 years from 1921 to 1971, a total of only 18 women were elected to the House of Commons, and only a dozen female "persons" were appointed to the Senate. By 1966, frustrated with male politicians' inaction on issues of concern to women, a coalition of women's organizations sent delegates to Ottawa to request a royal commission on the status of women. Their request, initially denied, was granted when an off-hand remark by one of the delegates, Laura Sabia, produced newspaper headlines forecasting a march on Ottawa by two million women.[31]

Appointed in 1967, the Commission's mandate was to recommend to the federal government what steps should be taken "to ensure for women equal opportunities with men in all aspects of Canadian society."[32] The Commission received 468 briefs and 1000 letters as women took advantage of the first invitation to express their views on their political, legal, and economic status. The Commission's assessment of women's participation in public life was stated bluntly in its final report:

In the decision-making positions, and most conspicuously in the government and Parliament of Canada, the presence of a mere handful of women is no more than a token acknowledgement of their right to be there. The voice of government is still a man's voice. The formulation of policies affecting the lives of all Canadians is still the prerogative of men. The absurdity of this situation was illustrated when debate in the House of Commons on a change in abortion law was conducted by 263 men and one woman.... The obstacles to genuine participation, when they lie in prejudice, in unequal family responsibility, or in financing a campaign, must be approached with a genuine determination to change the present imbalance.[33]

The Commission urged women to "show a greater determination to use their legal right to participate as citizens"[34] and made recommendations for changes that might facilitate their success. Specifically, they suggested increasing the number of women appointed to the Senate, abolishing the financial requirement for senators (ownership of land worth $4,000 or more and a net worth of the same amount), appointing more women judges, qualifying women for jury duty in all provinces that had not yet done so, and integrating the women's associations of political parties with the main party organizations. The Commission also made proposals concerning poverty, the family, education, the economy, Aboriginal women, reproductive choice, and a variety of other matters intended to improve women's opportunities and thereby expand their ability to participate in public life.

To oversee implementation of their 167 recommendations, the Commission proposed that federal and provincial governments appoint status of women councils, responsible to Parliament or the provincial legislatures and given sufficient funds and authority to make their work effective. Two years later, in 1972, concerned that the report had failed to produce action, women again began to organize nationally to press for implementation, forming the National Action Committee on the Status of Women (NAC). Like its nineteenth-century predecessor, the National Council of Women, NAC was a non-partisan umbrella group encompassing a range of political, religious, and community women's organizations. Also like its predecessor, NAC was to spend a large portion of its resources trying to persuade male politicians of the importance of women's concerns.

Despite the recommendations of the Royal Commission on the Status of Women in Canada, women still lacked an effective voice in government. The Canadian Advisory Council on the Status of Women and the Quebec Council on the Status of Women were appointed by their respective governments in 1973. But their power was limited because, contrary to the Royal Commission's recommendations, they did not report to Parliament or to the legislature directly but through a designated minister. Still, these and other provincial councils on the status of women did play significant roles by supporting research and public discussion on issues affecting women.

The Constitution Act, 1982 and its Aftermath

At the same time that women were urging change, the government of Pierre Trudeau was negotiating with the provinces to "patriate" the constitution. This meant reaching an agreement to transfer control over amending the constitution from Britain to Canada. This effort was the latest in a series of discussions and proposals since Confederation. In 1931, the Parliament of the United Kingdom had passed the *Statute of Westminster*, limiting the power of the British Parliament to pass legislation affecting the dominions, including Canada. There was one exception, however — the *British North America Act* itself. Amendments to the fundamental constitutional document of Canada could be made only by asking the British Parliament to pass legislation. This continued until the Parliament of the United Kingdom, at the request of the Parliament of Canada, passed the *Canada Act, 1982*, part of which was the *Constitution Act, 1982*, including the Charter and a procedure for amending the constitution in Canada.

It was not just a question of having the power to amend our own constitution. There was also a growing interest in constitutional protection of rights and freedoms. This was intensified by the October Crisis of 1970 and the use of the *War Measures Act* by the federal government to suspend civil liberties not only in Quebec but across the country. It was an extraordinary measure that underlined the absence of protection for fundamental rights and freedoms in Canada.

Following World War II and the United Nations Universal Declaration of Human Rights (1948), civil liberties had become more prominent in political discussions.[35] Parliament had passed the *Canadian Bill of Rights* (the Diefenbaker Bill of Rights) in 1960. It acknowledged certain human rights and fundamental freedoms, including "the right of the individual to equality before the law and the protection of the law. . . without discrimination by reason of race, national origin, colour, religion or sex. . .".[36] The *Canadian Bill of Rights*, however, is simply a law passed by Parliament — not an entrenched constitutional document. The *Canadian Bill of Rights* permits Parliament to pass laws inconsistent with its provisions; in fact, Parliament alone could repeal the Bill of Rights at any time. Its force was further restricted by the courts' reluctance to interpret it in any way that would limit the traditional supremacy of Parliament.[37]

As in other western traditions, civil liberties in Canada did not include concerns about women's inferior status. Rather, civil liberties were essentially about free speech, freedom of assembly, freedom of religion, and other such rights affecting men. To the degree that civil libertarians were concerned about discrimination against people based on their membership in a particular group — for example, race or religion — there was a tendency to overlook women as constituting such a group.[38]

In two notorious cases involving women's equality where the *Canadian Bill of Rights* was used, the Supreme Court of Canada upheld sex-based distinctions that discriminated against women.[39] Reaction to these cases played an important part in the later formulation of the equality provisions in the Charter.

In other areas, such as family law, women were finding the decisions of the courts and legislatures just as unsatisfactory. Without specific legislation entitling women to claim a share of matrimonial property, women lost such claims. For example, in 1974,[40] the Supreme Court of Canada refused an Alberta ranch wife, Irene Murdoch, any share in the ranch she had operated with her husband during 25 years of marriage. When the marriage ended, she was left with nothing because the ranch was registered in his name.

By this time, some provinces had started to develop new laws for dividing family property on marriage breakdown, and most had human rights codes in place, but it was clear that legal support for women's rights was still tenuous. It was also clear that both legislatures and courts were far from representative of the Canadian population and that they were failing to keep pace with women's growing expectations for equal treatment.

The women's liberation movement — like the civil rights movement in the United States and the nationalist movement in Quebec, and Aboriginal peoples in Canada and elsewhere — was demanding greater self-determination. Women wanted not only a voice but a hand in the decisions that affected their lives.

Outside the immediate framework of the constitutional debate, women were very active. The women's movement promoted public discussion and fostered activity through dozens of groups: women's centres, transition houses for battered women, rape crisis centres, and union caucuses. There were child-care activists, researchers, and advocates for legal rights, Aboriginal rights, reproductive rights, and every manner of social and political reform. The movement was not one voice, but many voices, not always unified and not always harmonious.

Despite this widespread activism, women are almost completely absent from the record of discussions regarding constitutional reform throughout the years 1967-1982, culminating in the very intense period between 1978 and 1982. For example, although many women appeared before the Special Joint Committee of the Senate and of the House of Commons on the Constitution of Canada in 1972, women as a group are mentioned in the Committee's report only as having "argued convincingly for equal treatment for women before and in the law and its administration."[41] In 1978, the Canadian Bar Association's Committee on the Constitution produced a 148-page document[42] containing three paragraphs on "Egalitarian Rights"[43] and none on women. (Perhaps this is not surprising, given that the Committee was composed of 12 men, had a two-man research staff, and consulted with 10 other people — all male.) Just as at Confederation, the process of constitutional debate throughout the 1970s was appropriated by a small group of men — federal and provincial politicians and bureaucrats and the legal establishment.

Through the councils on the status of women and the Women's Program of the Secretary of State (which provided funding to a range of women's groups), women were able to participate in public debate in Canada more than they could earlier. But many barriers remained. By 1987, women made up nearly 44 per cent of the labour force,[44] but full-time workers still earned only 65.9 per cent of what their male counterparts did.[45] Women also continued to carry the primary burden of childrearing and housework. For women, political parties were not avenues into the political system, but another set of stumbling blocks. It was not just that women had less time and money; they also had to confront continuing stereotyped notions of women as passive and supportive and of politics as a man's game. In the early 1980s, 70 per cent of local riding secretaries but only 8 per cent of political candidates were women.[46]

Constitutional reform gained momentum during the late 1970s and early 1980s.[47] When it couldn't reach agreement with the provinces, the federal government announced its intention to seek patriation of the constitution, with an entrenched bill of rights, on its own. A Special Joint Committee of the Senate and of the House of Commons held public meetings about the proposed charter of rights. Women's groups and many others made submissions. The committee recommended numerous amendments to the proposed charter, strengthening it considerably. Meanwhile, several provinces went to court to challenge the constitutionality of the federal government's intention to act; at the same time, groups representing Aboriginal peoples and provincial delegations were lobbying British parliamentarians to block the federal government's move by refusing to pass the proposed legislation.

The Supreme Court of Canada ruled that there was a constitutional convention requiring substantial agreement among the provinces before the *British North America Act* could be amended in a way that affected provincial powers.[48] This led to a series of pressured meetings and eventually the November Accord of 1981. Along the way to that Accord, Quebec was excluded, sowing the seeds that ripened into the Meech Lake Accord process. As well, the override clause (section 33) was added to the Charter at the insistence of several provinces.[49] After further battles and court rulings, agreement was reached between nine of the ten provinces and the federal government in November 1981. The total package agreed to in the November Accord included the Charter with the override clause, patriation, guaranteed provincial power over natural resources, and an amending formula.

In the November Accord, section 28 of the Charter (stating that the rights and freedoms in the Charter are guaranteed equally to male and female persons) was made subject to the section 33 override. Also, protection for Aboriginal rights was dropped. Intense and dramatic intervention by members of the public saved the priority of section 28 and the recognition of "existing" Aboriginal rights.[50]

At this point, there was hope that the process leading to the Charter represented the beginning, rather than the end, of women's participation in Canadian constitution-making. But this was not to be. On the very next occasion — the negotiations surrounding the Meech Lake Accord — the first ministers regressed to the classic closed process. And Prime Minister Brian Mulroney robustly defended this as a desirable method — in fact, as part of our "tradition". As *The Globe and Mail* reported:

> *He said he has no apologies to make for the marathon seven-day session he held to obtain the first ministers deal on Saturday night, and no regrets about the lack of public debate on the constitutional negotiations.*
>
> *"That's the way it had to be done. You're asking me if I have any regrets? None whatsoever."*
>
> *The Prime Minister said the private talks among the 11 men merely followed a tradition established by Canada's founding fathers. Citing the first talks held to achieve Confederation in 1867, Mr. Mulroney noted that Canada's constitutional architects, even the first prime minister, Sir John A. Macdonald, always conducted their most important debates in private, with plenty of liquor and unpublished remarks.*
>
> *"In Charlottetown, the boys arrived in a ship and spent a long time in places other than the library," Mr. Mulroney said, going on to cite other examples of hard-drinking, rough-talking sessions of constitution-building.*
>
> *"This is the way it was done. This is the way Confederation came about. There was no public debate; there was no great public hearings. It became a kind of tradition."*[51]

These remarks are worth noting for several reasons: (a) they use with approval, and even nostalgia, expressions like "the boys" and "the founding fathers"; (b) they clearly value an all-male club atmosphere as ideal for the exercise of constitution-building; and (c) they defend a process that excludes all women, and any serious consideration of women's interests, and will continue to do so for the foreseeable future, even if one or two women succeed in becoming first ministers.

Given the essentially geographical basis of our political system and all the obstacles to political participation, women's interests tend not to be represented through the electoral process. Further, the number of women among high-level bureaucrats and constitutional advisers is very low.[52] Thus, if women's interests are asserted at all in the context of an event such as a first ministers' conference on constitutional reform, it is from the outside. Likely, no one present **is** female, and no one feels any special responsibility to represent women's interests or perspectives. Women are on the outside and speaking after the fact, so their interests can be easily dismissed and characterized as "lobbying" by a "special interest group".[53] Expressions of women's concerns become trivialized as "single-issue politics". By contrast, the legitimacy of advocating regional interests is rarely questioned. Following the 1987 Meech Lake Accord process, lawyer Mary Eberts summarized the experience of women with constitutional change as follows:

> 1. *Constitutional decisions of great significance to women are made by men without notice to women, without consultation, and in the absence of any essential awareness of women's interests.*
>
> 2. *If there is to be any hope of reversing constitutional decisions made in this way, women must be prepared to act on very short notice and with a massive show of strength and solidarity. Circumstances dictate that they do so as volunteers, with but slender resources at their disposal, because women control none of the established, official processes of constitution making.*

3. *When action is taken in an attempt to reverse an initial [decision], decision-makers, in the short interval since its making, have developed an enormous attachment to the new-minted status quo, and a desire to maintain it almost for its own sake.*

4. *Resistance to women's concerns about constitutional initiatives range from the patronizing "Trust us" to ridicule, misrepresentation of women's position, and silencing. Women are also threatened that if they do not accept the deal as configured, the alternative will be worse.*

5. *Although women are told to speak with one voice, or run the risk of not being listened to, decision-makers also tell some women that, because of their regional, political or other characteristics, they have no right at all to be heard in the debate.*

6. *If any gains are made by women, these should be regarded as fragile, liable to be reversed without notice or consultation at the next meeting of male constitution-makers.*

7. *Gains for women, and equality guarantees in general, are particularly liable to be sacrificed in the interests of provincial powers.*[54]

Still, women did have more influence on the constitutional change leading to the Charter than was the case at any other stage in Canadian history. And it is no coincidence that the Charter is the first Canadian constitutional document that expressly recognizes gender.

Discussion Questions

1. Discuss the role of Aboriginal and European women in pre-Confederation times.

2. Were there any "Mothers of Confederation"?

3. Discuss suffrage for women in post-Confederation times.

4. What did the Royal Commission on the Status of Women in Canada say about women's participation in public life? If the Commission were reporting today, what should it say?

5. Discuss the evolution of human rights and sex equality laws in Canada. What role did women have in these achievements? List some of the obstacles women have faced in seeking these goals.

6. How were women virtually excluded from the constitutional process?

Conclusion

Women's interest in the constitution has grown since the passage of the equality provisions in the Charter in 1982. But it is not only the equality provisions, or even the Charter itself, that make the subject "Women and the Constitution" particularly compelling. It is the range of possibilities that women's participation in constitutional change, and a feminist perspective on the constitution as a whole, can open up. The process leading to the Charter included women in a new way, though still at the margins. To some extent, some women may feel more part of the constitution now as a result. Political scientist Alan Cairns put it this way:

The Charter brought new groups into the constitutional order or, as in the case of aboriginals, enhanced a pre-existing constitutional status. It bypassed governments and spoke directly to Canadians by defining them as bearers of rights, as well as by according specific constitutional recognition to women, aboriginals, official language minority populations, ethnic groups through the vehicle of multiculturalism, and to those social categories explicitly listed in the equality rights section of the Charter. The Charter thus reduced the relative status of governments and strengthened that of the citizens who received constitutional encouragement to think of themselves as constitutional actors.[1]

This insight is important but must be understood in a larger context. First, women, or men who fall into the other "social categories" listed in section 15, are not simply "Charter Canadians", with no particular interest in **other** aspects of the Constitution. Second, women (or such men) are not simply a "special interest group" whose assertions as women or as, for example, persons with disabilities, are an understandable manifestation of self-interest (and therefore dismissable). Women are not a "lobby group". This characterization: (a) implicitly but falsely lumps women with true lobbyists in pursuit of special interests such as the Canadian Manufacturers' Association or the Bowen Island Ratepayers Association; (b) ignores the fact that women form a majority of the population; (c) accepts the predefined terms of the debate, whereby regional interests are legitimately at the table, but the interests of people defined in other ways (e.g., by gender or by Aboriginal status) are not.

Rather, the articulation of women's interests can and should be seen as an aspect of ordinary good citizenship. Feminist political scientist Iris Young points out the error of the proposition that "all citizens should assume the same impartial, general point of view transcending all particular interests, perspectives and experiences" in exercising their citizenship. She writes:

But such an impartial general perspective is a myth. People necessarily and properly consider public issues in terms influenced by their situated experience and perception of social relations.

Different social groups have different needs, cultures, histories, experiences, and perceptions of social relations which influence their interpretation of the meaning and consequences of policy proposals and influence the form of their political reasoning. These differences in political interpretation are not merely or even primarily a result of differing or conflicting interests, for groups have differing interpretations even when they seek to promote justice and not merely their own self-regarding ends. In a society where some groups are privileged while others are oppressed, insisting that as citizens persons should leave behind their particular affiliations and experiences to adopt a general point of view serves only to reinforce that privilege; for the perspectives and interests of the privileged will tend to dominate this unified public, marginalizing or silencing those of other groups.[2]

This approach reinforces the theme running through our review of Women and the Constitution: women are severely under-represented in our government, in our judiciary, and in the upper reaches of our public service. Thus, constitutional rules are made, interpreted, and implemented without much participation by women. Law professor Beverley Baines has observed that it is "taken for granted that men can and should represent the interests of women, not just politically but constitutionally".[3] We think it should not be taken for granted any longer.

Before moving on to discuss possible ways to improve representation and, therefore, participation in constitution-making, two points should be noted. First, the definition of "politics" has been heavily slanted toward what men do, in male-created structures such as political parties and legislatures, and away from what women do, in community organizations and women's groups.[4] So the actual participation rate of women in politics is therefore much higher than the standard statistics would suggest. Unfortunately, the male structures hold the power and the female ones do not.

Second, simply increasing women's participation in the existing political party system, without envisioning changes in that system, is not enough. Political scientist Jill Vickers argues:
One central question we must ask is whether we believe the state can ever be transformed into either a neutral agency for the common good or one in which there can be a balance of power between male and female interests. . . . The answer to this basic question is far from clear. But it would help us to determine if we want to be "inside" or to remain "outside", exercising whatever leverage we have but resolutely refusing to legitimize institutions we believe can never be satisfactorily transformed.[5]

In the end, Vickers takes an agnostic (or, as she describes it, "mugwumpish") position on the central question she poses. We do not dispute the wisdom, at this stage, of leaving one's "mug" on one side of the fence and one's "wump" on the other. However, in looking at the question in a constitutional context, one would have to ask what has **non**-participation done for women?.

Assuming that participation is worth women's while, what can be done to increase it? Starting with the political process, because it is most directly connected with the making of constitutional change, many possibilities may be explored. In its *Brief to the Royal Commission on Electoral Reform and Party Financing*[6] in June 1990, the Canadian Advisory Council on the Status of

Conclusion

Women made a number of recommendations aimed at reducing obstacles to women's participation. They included:
- lowering financial barriers by requiring employers to give employees unpaid leaves of absence to seek nomination or election, or to hold office (for six years), and by moving to a system of election financing that is wholly funded out of public money and does not require private fundraising;
- creating incentives to nominate women, raising reimbursement for election expenses of women candidates, and — when women comprise at least 50 per cent of the candidates list — rewarding parties with a higher level of reimbursement;
- removing barriers in the nomination process, regulating nomination compaigns under the *Canada Elections Act,* and making expenses at the nomination stage eligible for partial reimbursement with women candidates' expenses being reimbursed at a higher level;
- considering the feasibility of methods such as proportional representation or dual-member, male-female constituencies, with the goal of achieving equality of representation.

Despite the efforts of the Canadian Advisory Council on the Status of Women and other organizations,[7] it is still rare for women or men in "mainstream" discussions about the political process to identify the under-representation of women as a problem. The mention of methods to improve women's representation, such as those referred to above or others, such as a Senate in which women would make up 50 per cent of Senators, is regarded as a distraction from the really important issues facing the country. Of course, the future of Quebec in Canada and of self-government for First Nations people are of critical importance. But certainly, if a group consisting of 51 per cent of the population happened to be concentrated in one geographic area yet was represented in Parliament by only 13.5 per cent of the MPs, this would be identified as a significant problem. Law professor Christine Boyle[8] explores this:

Imagine a country in which all or most of the women, but not the men, lived in one geographical area — for example, Ontario. One can then examine the laws applying to and the economic position of "Ontarians" from a neutral standpoint. It will be found that the position of Ontarians is not good in Canadian society. They have been systematically discriminated against throughout their history; for example, their property was taken from them without compensation, they had no rights to their children, enfranchisement was ridiculed and bitterly opposed, and they still rarely sit in Parliament or on the bench. They are subjected to assault and sexual abuse by non-Ontarians, and they largely work at menial tasks for which they are paid much less than non-Ontarians, or nothing. In addition, they are depicted ever more widely by various media as being less than human, as objects for the sexual gratification of non-Ontarians. One has only to attempt such an account to realize that there exist two fundamentally different groups in Canada (and, of course, elsewhere). It is submitted that an electoral system which does not reflect any confrontation of that fact is inadequate.[9]

Women are dispersed (more or less evenly) throughout the country, so that tinkering with electoral boundaries will not do anything for women as such. That does not mean, however, that the problem disappears or that we should give up on the task of finding a solution. One of the fundamental underlying assumptions in our constitution is, as has been discussed here, that "Geography is Destiny". This has many consequences. The intense focus on federal-provincial relations, and on territorial representation, are two examples. The federalism model recognizes geographic and some kinds of cultural diversity, but makes invisible other kinds of diversity such as gender.

While women in Canada may have different views about many constitutional issues (and why not?), from a feminist perspective it is important to question the territorial (originally property-based) model that works so well to keep women out of the process.

Whether within our own communities or in the Canadian community as a whole, women can also question a second fundamental underlying assumption of the Canadian constitution: that gender is not an issue. As we have seen, there was no mention of gender or women in the parts of the Canadian constitution that preceded the Charter. (In fact, there is no reference to the Canadian people at all in the *British North America Act* except in the context of counting them, taxing them, or determining their eligibility for office.) Yet in some ways, through omission, the Canadian constitution does embody principles defining the relationship between women and men. For example, the principle that prohibits the state from intruding on individual liberties without legal authority enshrines the notion that "A man's home is his castle". Until recently, this was strictly adhered to with respect to domestic violence, which meant that wife battering could continue as a "private matter". It must also be remembered that at common law, discrimination of any sort — racial, religious, sexual — was permitted in most circumstances. This made it necessary to enact human rights legislation in every Canadian jurisdiction to deal with discrimination in employment, housing, and other matters. Not only is the legislation very recent, but it was not until the 1980s that the courts recognized these rights as reflecting fundamental values and therefore to be given serious interpretation.

What the Charter does, in recognizing gender as an issue and entrenching rights to equality for women, is an enormous departure from what has gone before. It is also a departure from much of what still goes on in Canadian society today, where "women's issues" appear only fleetingly, and at the margins, of the national agenda. Trying to implement the Charter equality rights is like trying to divert a stream from its established channel. The stream always tries to return to its habitual course.

One advantage that Canadian women have in this project is that the Canadian constitution not only defines the relationship between the individual and the state, and between various parts of the state, it also includes principles defining the relationships between various collectivities or groups of people. In particular, the relationships between Aboriginal peoples and those who have arrived in Canada more recently,[10] between francophones and anglophones,[11] and between Roman Catholics and Protestants[12] are visibly recognized. This is one of the important respects in which our constitution (and our society) is different from that of the United States. From the outset, we understood the importance of collective interests and have recognized some collective rights in the constitution. This has implications in many areas. For instance, the meaning of "equality" under section 15 of the *Canadian Charter of Rights and Freedoms* is developing in a

Conclusion

less individualistic direction than has been the case under the equivalent provision in the United States Constitution. This may be seen in the *Andrews* [13] case, which recognizes that the disadvantage experienced by **groups** (such as racial or religious minorities, women, or persons with disabilities) will be the measure of equality.

It might be desirable, then, for women to be seen as the kind of group that can be afforded rights recognized in international law such as the right to self-determination. One difficulty, because of the "Geography is Destiny" assumption, is women's lack of a territorial base. Another problem, ironically, is the large size of the group "women". The number and diversity of women can make it easy to divide women into sub-groups and thereby defeat measures that would enhance the position of women as a whole. Finally, the model of group rights has not been designed with women in mind and, as usual with such models, it may need more alteration than it can bear to make it fit. However, whether or not women can be seen as a group or collective with a legitimate claim to self-determination in the same way as a group of men and women of common ethnic origin and territorial location, the respect for diversity that helps claims for collective rights also helps women's claims. The converse is also true: the attention to identifying and eradicating systematic subordination not only helps women, it helps groups of women and men subordinated because of their race or other factors.

The "equality project" of women should include but not be limited to a constitutional focus. In some ways, the constitution of a country embodies its values, its goals, as well as its rules. Only to a limited extent does it create those values and goals. It seems most accurate to say that it states them in an authoritative way and may, therefore, enhance them. The Canadian constitution, as interpreted in the courts, is just beginning to recognize the importance of equality for women in our laws and social arrangements.

In this paper, we have attempted to begin what we think should be a companion project — turning the principle of equality for women inward on the Canadian constitution, so that equality becomes a governing principle of the constitution itself.

Notes

Introduction

1. *Schachter v. Canada* (1988), 52 D.L.R. (4th) 525, 18 F.T.R. 199, 3 F.C. 515 (T.D.), (1990) 66 D.L.R. (4th) 635 (C.A.).

2. [Editor's note: The case is under reserve by the Supreme Court of Canada. Subsequent amendments to the *Unemployment Insurance Act* provided for 10 weeks of parental leave benefits for adoptive parents and birth parents (a reduction for adoptive parents), and up to 25 weeks maximum for birth mothers.]

3. *Brooks v. Canada Safeway Ltd.*, [1989] 4 W.W.R. 193, 59 D.L.R. (4th) 321, 1 S.C.R. 1219.

4. *Ibid.*, W.W.R. at 208.

5. *Bliss v. Attorney General of Canada*, [1979] 1 S.C.R. 183, [1978] 6 W.W.R. 711, 92 D.L.R. (3d) 417.

6. *Brooks v. Canada Safeway Ltd.*, *supra*, note 3 at 212.

What is a Constitution?

1. J.A. Corry, "The Uses of a Constitution", *Special Lectures of the Law Society of Upper Canada 1978* (Toronto: Richard DeBoo, 1978), p. 4.

2. K.C. Wheare, *Modern Constitutions* (London: Oxford University Press, 1966), pp. 50-51.

3. United States constitutional jurisprudence reflects this understanding. In 1819, Chief Justice Marshall of the U.S. Supreme Court wrote:

    The government proceeds directly from the people; ... In form and in substance it emanates from them. Its powers are granted by them, and are to be exercised directly on them, and for their benefit....It is the government of all; its powers are delegated by all; it represents all, and acts for all. (McCulloch v. Maryland, 4 Wheaton 316.)

4. See George Woodcock, *The Century That Made Us: Canada 1814-1914* (Don Mills, Ont.: Oxford University Press, 1989), p. 8, and chapters 4 and 5.

5. Alan C. Cairns and Douglas Williams, eds., *Constitution, Government, and Society in Canada: Selected Essays* (Toronto: McClelland and Stewart, 1988), p. 27.

6. Ronald L. Watts, "The American Constitution in Comparative Perspective: A Comparison of Federalism in the United States and Canada", *Journal of American History*, vol. 74 (1987), pp. 769-771.

7. Interview on CBC Television, "The Journal", June 20, 1990.

What is a Feminist Perspective?

1. *Re Section 24 of the B.N.A. Act*, [1928] 4 D.L.R. 98.

2. *Edwards v. A.G. Can.*, [1930] A.C. 124, [1929] 3 W.W.R. 479, (1930) 1. D.L.R. 98 (P.C.).

3. The Privy Council said: "The word 'person' as above mentioned may include members of both sexes, and to those who ask why the word should include females, the obvious answer is why should it not." *Ibid.*

4. *Ibid.*, at D.L.R. 106-107.

What is the Canadian Constitution?

1. These are the documents listed in s. 52(2) of the *Constitution Act, 1982*, which reads: "The Constitution of Canada includes (a) the *Canada Act 1982*, including this Act; (b) the Acts and orders referred to in the schedule, and (c) any amendment to any Act or order referred to in paragraph (a) or (b)." The *Constitution Act, 1982* is itself part of the *Canada Act 1982*, U.K. 1982, c. 11, being Schedule B to it.

2. R.S.C. 1985, App. II, No. 1.

3. Jack Woodward, *Native Law* (Toronto: Carswell, 1989), p. 63.

4. *Calder v. A.G.B.C.* (1973), 34 D.L.R. (3d) 145 at 203, per Hall, J. quoted in Woodward, *ibid.*, pp. 75-76.

5. Peter W. Hogg, *Constitutional Law of Canada*, 2nd ed. (Toronto: Carswell, 1985), p. 12.

6. *Reference re Amendment of the Constitution of Canada (Nos. 1, 2, 3)] Patriation Reference Case* (1981), 125 D.L.R. (3d) 1, [1981] 1 S.C.R. 753, [1981] 6 W.W.R. 1 at D.L.R. 84.

7. *Re Objection by Quebec to Resolution to Amend the Constitution*, [1982] 2 S.C.R. 793.

8. Eugene A. Forsey, "The Courts and the Conventions of the Constitution" (1984), 33 U.N.B.L.J. 11 at 41.

9. Hogg, *supra*, note 5, p. 212.

10. Though this is happenstance, because the English Crown is inherited by primogeniture, i.e., it passes to the eldest male in the direct line of the monarch. Thus, Princess Anne would only ever become Queen if Prince Charles, as well as his sons, Prince Andrew, Prince Edward, and any sons they might have had, were all to predecease her. Still, the English system was more egalitarian than that in France, which precluded women from inheriting the Crown altogether.

11. The cabinet as such is not mentioned in the constitution, but the Privy Council is established under it, and mandated to "aid and advise in the Government of Canada" (see s. 11 of the *Constitution Act, 1867*). All cabinet ministers are appointed to the Privy Council, but many Privy Councillors are not members of the cabinet; rather, they are honourary appointees or past Cabinet ministers, since appointments are for life. The cabinet is the active part of the Privy Council.

12. Canada, Task Force on Barriers to Women in the Public Service, *Beneath the Veneer: Report of the Task Force on Barriers to Women in the Public Service* (Ottawa: 1990), vol. 1, p. 115.

13. Sylvia B. Bashevkin, *Toeing the Lines: Women and Party Politics in English Canada* (Toronto: University of Toronto Press, 1985), p. 159.

14. Hogg, *supra*, note 5, p. 197, footnote 27.

15. These notions find pervasive expression, sometimes semi-consciously. For example, an editorial cartoon run during the 1989 New Democratic Party (NDP) leadership convention showed a boxing match between two puny males, one of whom was carrying a purse and had his gloves over his face saying "Ouch!", in front of a sign reading "N.D.P. HEAVYWEIGHT TRYOUTS". The message, of course, is that pugilistic strength is a *sine qua non* of "leadership", and that someone who carries a purse is clearly lacking "the right stuff". See *The Globe and Mail*, June 24, 1989, p. D2; cartoon by "CAM", *Regina Leader Post*.

16. Until that date, appeals to the Judicial Committee of the Privy Council of the United Kingdom were possible. In fact, appeals to the Privy Council are still possible for cases "commenced" prior to December 23, 1949 (likely, by this time, an empty category).

17. The Supreme Court **must** hear some appeals (for example, from constitutional references brought by provincial governments to their Courts of Appeal and in criminal cases where a judge of a province's Court of Appeal has dissented on a question of law), but in most instances it selects the cases it hears on the basis of their national importance.

18. Because provinces have a right to appeal provincial reference cases to the Supreme Court of Canada, the provinces have a means of obtaining the opinion of that Court on questions that trouble them: *Supreme Court Act*, section 37. This was the mechanism used in the *Patriation Reference* case, *supra*, note 6.

19. *Constitution Act, 1871*, R.S.C. 1970, Appendix II, No. 11, s. 4.

20. *Constitution Act, 1867*, s. 99. The Governor General may remove a judge from office, on the request of the Senate and House of Commons. The Canadian Judicial Council makes recommendations with respect to particular instances of alleged judicial misconduct, and may hold hearings (as it has done in the allegations against members of the Nova Scotia Court of Appeal in connection with the Donald Marshall case).

21. Peter H. Russell and Jacob S. Ziegel, "Federal Judicial Appointments: An Appraisal of the First Mulroney Government's Appointments", May 1989, Draft Paper for the Canadian Association of Law Teachers.

22. *Dame Langstaff v. The Bar of the Province of Quebec* (1915), 47 Q.S.C. 131 at 139-140.

23. Russell and Ziegel, *supra*, note 21.

Notes

24. What this means in practice is not entirely clear, as shown by the controversy in 1981 over the comments of former B.C. Supreme Court Justice Thomas Berger regarding the omission of Aboriginal peoples' rights from the Constitution. (See "Report and Record of the Committee of Investigation into the Conduct of the Hon. Mr. Justice Berger and Resolution of the Canadian Judicial Council", (1983) 28 *McGill Law Journal* 378.) For an interview with Berger discussing the issue see Garry Sturgess and Philip Chubb, eds., *Judging the World: Law and Politics in the World's Leading Courts* (Toronto: Butterworths, 1988), pp. 404-409.

    A recent example of a similar debate may be found in the reaction to a lecture delivered by Madam Justice Bertha Wilson in 1990 ("Will Women Judges Really Make a Difference?", The Fourth Annual Barbara Betcherman Memorial Lecture, Osgoode Hall Law School, February 8, 1990). Clearly, judges are expected to stay away from partisan politics and from comment on pending litigation or issues in it. However, a respectable body of opinion holds that it is a different matter for a judge to comment on issues of overwhelming public importance affecting citizens whose interests have been overlooked in the political process.

25. Wilson, *ibid.*

26. *R. v. Lavallée*, [1990] 4 W.W.R. 1 (S.C.C.).

27. As Peter Hogg argues, in *Constitutional Law of Canada, supra*, note 5, the following features of the *British North America Act* indicate an intention to create a strong central government: the federal Parliament has the residual power to legislate when a matter has not been assigned as either federal or provincial (s. 91); the federal government was given the "trade and commerce" power without qualification (s. 91(2)), as well as powers over banking (s. 91(15)), marriage and divorce (s. 91(26)), criminal law (s. 91(27)), and penitentiaries (s. 91(28)), although the states were given these powers under the U.S. constitution; the federal government was made fiscally dominant through its power to levy both direct and indirect taxation. As well, in some ways the provinces were legislatively subordinate to the federal government: the federal government was given the power to invalidate ("disallow") provincial statutes (s. 90); the federal government appoints the Lieutenant Governor of each province (s. 58) as well as the superior, district, and county courts of the provinces (s. 96); the federal government could bring local works under exclusive federal legislative jurisdiction simply by declaring them to be "for the general advantage of Canada" (ss. 91(29) and 92(10(c)).

28. However, the central government has more extensive taxing powers. By virtue of section 91(3), the federal government has the power to raise money "by any mode or system of taxation". The provincial governments may impose "direct" taxes (s. 92(2)) and licence fees (s. 92(9)). The difference in taxing powers has led to such devices as the federal-provincial cost-sharing agreements in areas including medical services and education.

29. The federal government was given: (a) the power to make criminal law; (b) the responsibility for penitentiaries; (c) the power to set up the Supreme Court of Canada (s. 101) and, by implication, the right to appoint judges to that court; and (d) the power to appoint judges to the superior courts in the provinces (s. 96). The provinces were given control of the administration of justice, the organization of provincial courts, civil procedure, and reformatory prisons. Each province was to maintain its existing body of laws (s. 129), and the continuation of Quebec's distinctive civil law system was thus guaranteed.

30. *Constitution Act, 1867*, s. 95 refers to immigration and agriculture; s. 92A(2) and 92A(3) refer to natural resources-shared jurisdiction; and s. 94A refers to old age pensions.

31. Section 23 of the *Manitoba Act, 1870*. The Manitoba legislature purported to overrule this section in enacting its *Official Language Act* in 1890. The *Official Language Act* was held invalid by courts on several occasions over the years, but the court rulings were ignored by the governments. Eventually, in *A.G. Man. v. Forest* [1979] 2 S.C.R. 1032, the Supreme Court of Canada confirmed the invalidity and that the *Manitoba Act* did require statutes to be written in both English and French. By 1984 little progress had been made in producing bilingual statutes, and the Supreme Court of Canada held in *Reference re Language Rights under the Manitoba Act, 1870*, [1985] 1 S.C.R. 721, 19 D.L.R. (4th) 1 that the English-only statutes were invalid, but that the government could have time to translate them.

32. S. 93; see also similar provisions in the Acts admitting Manitoba, Alberta, Saskatchewan, and Newfoundland.

33. *Constitution Act, 1867*, by the *Constitution Act, 1940*, 3-4 Geo. VI, c. 36 (U.K.).

34. S. 94A, *Constitution Act, 1867*, added by the *Constitution Act, 1964*, 12-13 Eliz. II, c. 73 (U.K.).

35. *Johanneson v. West St. Paul*, [1952] 1 S.C.R. 292.

36. See, for example, *Westendorp v. The Queen*, [1983] 1 S.C.R. 43, where a City of Calgary bylaw against street soliciting for the purposes of prostitution was found to be an invasion of the federal criminal law power.

37. After 1949, some amendments were possible in Canada: *Constitution Act, 1867*, s. 91(1) Canadian Constitution and s. 92(1) Provincial Constitution.

38. Although the number did not have to include Quebec, according to the Supreme Court of Canada, *Re Objection by Quebec to Resolution to Amend the Constitution*, supra, note 7.

39. Although Hogg, *supra*, note 5, argues that this provision (s. 42(1)(d)) is probably ineffective because rules regarding the composition of the Supreme Court of Canada are not contained in the Constitution of Canada; rather, they are in the *Supreme Court Act*, a federal statute.

40. Although not earlier than one year from the first resolution agreeing to the amendment, unless all provinces and the federal government have passed resolutions one way or the other before that time — section 39(1).

41. Even if there are dissents, if the requisite majority is obtained the amendment will take effect and apply across the country. There is one exception provided for in section 38(2), which allows a province to opt out of an amendment that "derogates from the legislative powers, the proprietary rights or any other rights or privileges of the legislature or government of a province...". Obviously, no more than three provinces representing less than 50 per cent of the population could choose to opt out of an amendment — otherwise, it could not pass. Under section 40, provinces that opt out of amendments where there is a transfer of provincial legislative powers relating to education or other cultural matters are entitled to "reasonable compensation" from the federal government so that, in those areas, provinces are not faced with a financial disincentive to retaining jurisdiction.

42. Specifically, "the right of a province to a number of members in the House of Commons not less than the number of Senators by which the province is entitled to be represented at the time this Part comes into force" — s. 41(b).

Notes

43. As with respect to section 42 (1) (d) discussed *supra*, note 39, Hogg, (*supra*, note 5), argues that this provision (s. 41(d)) is probably ineffective because rules regarding the composition of the Supreme Court of Canada are not contained in the Constitution of Canada; rather, they are in the *Supreme Court Act*, a federal statute.

44. Section 45 is subject to section 41, which requires in paragraph (a) that amendments relating to the office of the Lieutenant Governor have unanimous approval of all provinces and the federal government.

45. For example, the Australian constitution may be amended by a simple majority in both houses of the federal Parliament, subject to approval by referendum. The referendum must pass by a majority of citizens overall, and it must pass in a majority of the states. In the United States, the requirement is for approval by two-thirds majorities in both the House of Representatives and the Senate, and by the legislatures of three-quarters of the states or constitutional conventions in three-quarters of the states.

46. Quebec historically insisted upon a veto over constitutional change. When the resolutions bringing about the *Canada Act, 1982* went forward without Quebec's approval, this led to strong demands by Quebec for a veto in the negotiations leading to the Meech Lake Accord. This demand was picked up by other provinces, leading to the result that every province now has a veto over many important types of constitutional amendment. As well, the nine provinces that did agree to the *Canada Act, 1982* were able to obtain major concessions from the federal government, such as the unanimity requirement, in return for their agreement to other aspects of the package.

47. Under section 38 of the *Constitution Act, 1982*, this would require resolutions passed by at least two-thirds of the provinces that have at least 50 per cent of the population, plus the Parliament of Canada.

48. *Reference re Manitoba Language Rights*, [1985] 1 S.C.R. 721 at 745.

49. This is one of the most obvious differences between the Canadian constitution and that of the United States. There, the rights are stated in absolute terms and there is no equivalent to section 1. However, the U.S. courts have developed a method for permitting governments to impose reasonable limits on rights. It is done through defining the rights in a way that permits them to be exercised only in a limited sphere.

50. *Ref. re Criminal Code, Ss. 193 and 195.1 (1)(c)*, [1990] 1 S.C.R. 1123 4 W.W.R. 481 at 556.

51. *Irwin Toy Ltd. v. Que. (A.-G.)*, [1989] 1 S.C.R. 927, 58 D.L.R. (4th) 577. In *Rocket v. Royal College of Dental Surgeons of Ontario* ([1990] 2 S. C. R. 232), the Supreme Court of Canada stated that the fact that the expression is for commercial purposes may be taken into account when doing the section 1 analysis and noted that "...restrictions on expression of this kind might be easier to justify than other infringements of s.2(b)".

52. *Canadian Newspapers Co. v. Canada (Attorney General)* (1988), 43 C.C.C. (3d) 24, 52 D.L.R. (4th) 690, [1988] 2 S.C.R. 122.

53. *Edwards Books & Art Ltd. v. The Queen*, [1986] 2 S.C.R. 713, (1986), 35 D.L.R. (4th) 1, 30 C.C.C. (3d) 385, at S.C.R. 779:

> *In interpreting and applying the Charter I believe that the courts must be cautious to ensure that it does not simply become an instrument of better situated individuals to roll back legislation which has as its object the improvement of the condition of less advantaged persons.*

54. Canadian Advisory Council on the Status of Women, *Recommendations*, "Canadian Judicial Education Centre", Sept. 1986, D1.5; and "Wife Battering: Improving the Response of the Criminal Justice System", Sept. 1987, F1.9.

55. It was used by the government of Saskatchewan when it enacted back-to-work legislation against provincial public employees (*The SGEU Dispute Settlement Act*, S.S. 1984-85-86, c. 111). Just after the Charter became effective, the Quebec government used it to immunize every possible provincial statute from the Charter, as a political protest against Quebec's exclusion from the constitutional agreement. As well, the Quebec government passed laws in 1989 requiring exterior signs to be in French only, after the Supreme Court of Canada had struck down similar legislation. The Supreme Court of Canada found that the sign laws infringed the right to freedom of expression under section 2(b) of the Charter: *Devine v. Quebec (Attorney General)* (1988), 90 N.R. 48; *Ford v. Quebec (Attorney General)* (1988), 2 S.C.R. 712, 90 N.R. 84, 54 D.L.R. (4th) 577. Subsequently, the Quebec government passed legislation similar to that which had been struck down, and invoked section 33 of the Charter to preclude judicial review of that legislation.

56. In particular, the Supreme Court of Canada's approach to the abortion issue in *R. v. Morgentaler*, [1988] 1 S.C.R. 30.

57. Some women's organizations in Quebec, for example, the Conseil du statut de la femme (CSF) and the Fédération des femmes du Quebec (FFQ), did not share these concerns about the omission of section 28, although the FFQ reached a joint position with the National Action Committee on the Status of Women (NAC) regarding an amendment on this point. For an overview of the positions and discussion of women's groups regarding the Meech Lake Accord, see Barbara Roberts, *Smooth Sailing or Storm Warning? Canadian and Quebec Women's Groups on the Meech Lake Accord* (Ottawa: Canadian Research Institute for the Advancement of Women, 1989). For a discussion of the arguments about the Meech Lake Accord and its potential effects on women's equality, see L. Smith, "The Distinct Society Clause in the Meech Lake Accord: Could It Affect Equality Rights for Women?", in *Competing Constitutional Visions: The Meech Lake Accord*, ed. K.E. Swinton and C.J. Rogerson (Toronto: Carswell, 1988).

58. Cases: For example, the Court Challenges Fund, administered by the Human Rights Centre at the University of Ottawa, is available for some cases in the federal sphere. [Editor's note: The Court Challenges Fund was abolished by the federal government in February 1992.]

    Advocacy groups: For example, the Women's Legal Education and Action Fund (LEAF) and the Canadian Disability Rights Council.

59. This categorization is adopted from Donna Greschner, "A Walk Through the Charter", in *Charter of Rights: Who Cares? A Post-Conference Recap,* Regina Business and Professional Women's Club (Regina: 1985).

60. Given the exclusion or segregation of women in many established religions, on the whole it seems fair to see the absence of an official state religion as favouring women's equality.

Notes

61. In three cases involving the right to strike and to bargain collectively for trade unions, the Court decided that the *Charter* right does not protect those activities. Rather, it protects the right to form an association, maintain it, and participate in its lawful activities. It does not guarantee the right to participate in particular activity that would give an association meaningful existence: *Reference re Public Service Employee Relations Act, Labour Relations Act and Police Officers Collective Bargaining Act (1987), 38 D.L.R. (4th) 161, [1987] 1 S.C.R. 313; Public Service Alliance of Canada et al. v. The Queen in right of Canada et al. (1987), 38 D.L.R. (4th) 249, [1987] 1 S.C.R. 424; Saskatchewan (Government) et al. v. Retail, Wholesale & Department Store Union, Locals 544, 496, 635 and 955 et al.* (1987), 38 D.L.R. (4th) 277, [1987] 1 S.C.R. 460.

62. The leading test case on this issue is *Tomen v. F.W.T.A.O.* (1989), 70 O.R. (2d) 48 (C.A.), which concerns a challenge to the status of the women's elementary teachers associations in Ontario. An oversimplified understanding of equality can lead to the conclusion that all single-sex organizations must be treated alike, so that the business club that excludes women has to fall under the same rule as the sexual assault survivors' support group that excludes men. This fails to take account of the differing life circumstances of men and women in our society, and of the fact that equality cannot be created simply by adding the same amount to both sides of a scale.

63. *R. v. Keegstra*, [1990] 3 S.C.R. 697.

64. *R. v. Butler*, File no. 22191, Feb. 27, 1992. [Editor's note: The Court upheld s. 163 of the *Criminal Code* in its February 1992 decision.]

65. *Canadian Newspapers Co. v. Canada (Attorney General)*, *supra*, note 52. On the other hand, provisions restricting access to certain types of information in matrimonial cases were struck down in *Edmonton Journal v. Alta. (A.G.)* (1990) 1 W.W.R. 577 (S.C.C.).

66. Women with disabilities still face access problems in the exercise of their right to vote, but an explicit disqualification of some disabled persons from voting (those who were restrained of liberty of movement or deprived of management of their property by reason of mental disease) was struck down in 1988 (*Canadian Disability Rights Council v. Canada* (1988), 21 F.T.R. 268 (T.D.)). Women in prison, a disproportionate number of whom are First Nations women, are also disqualified from voting under various federal and provincial statutes. There have been mixed results in prisoners' right to vote cases, some courts finding that section 1 justifies denying prisoners the franchise, and others finding that the right to vote is so fundamental that the denial cannot be justified. See, for example, *Grondin v. Ontario (Attorney General)* (1988), 65 O.R. (2d) 427 (H.C.J.), finding the disqualification of prisoners from voting in provincial elections unjustified, and *Sauvé v. Canada (Attorney General)* (1988), 66 O.R. (2nd) 234, 53 D.L.R. (4th) 595 (Ont. H.C.J.), finding the disqualification in federal elections justified. The Manitoba Court of Appeal, in *Badger v. Canada (Attorney General)*, [1989] 1 W.W.R. 216 came to the same conclusion, i.e., the federal legislation is justified in excluding inmates from voting.

67. In *Re Hoogbruin et al. and Attorney General of British Columbia et al.* (1985), 24 D.L.R. (4th) 718, [1986] 2 W.W.R. 700, 70 B.C.L.R. 1 (C.A.), the court said that the British Columbia *Election Act*, R.S.B.C. 1979, c. 103, contravened section 3 in failing to provide a mechanism for absentee voting for those otherwise entitled to vote in a provincial election.

68. *Dixon v. Attorney General of British Columbia* (1989), 35 B.C.L.R. (2d) 273. McLachlin, C.J.S.C. (as she then was) held that equality of voting power is fundamentally important in assessing electoral boundaries, and the boundaries in British Columbia were drawn in a manner that contravened section 3, because there were such large discrepancies between the number of voters in the largest suburban ridings and in the smallest rural ridings. At the extremes, the vote of a citizen in Atlin (rural) was worth 12.4 times the vote of a citizen in Surrey-Newton (suburban). However, in *Reference re Electoral Boundaries Commission Act, ss. 14, 20 (Sask.)* (1991), 81 D.L.R. (4th) 16, the Supreme Court, in a decision written by McLachlin J., upheld a distribution of seats with considerable discrepancy between urban and rural ridings, on the basis that the issue was effective representation, not numerical equivalence.

69. *Singh et al. v. Minister of Employment and Immigration* (1985), 17 D.L.R. (4th) 422, [1985] 1 S.C.R. 177.

70. *Reference re Section 94(2) of the Motor Vehicle Act R.S.B.C. 1979* (1985), 23 C.C.C. (3d) 289, 24 D.L.R. (4th) 536, [1985] 2 S.C.R. 486.

71. *Irwin Toy Ltd. v. Quebec (A.G.)*. (1989) 1 S.C.R. 927.

72. The claim asserted in *Borowski v. Attorney General for Canada*, [1989] 1 S.C.R. 342, 57 D.L.R. (4th) 231, 3 W.W.R. 97 was that the fetus has the right to life, liberty, and security of the person, and that therefore section 251 of the *Criminal Code* (as it then was) should be struck down as unconstitutional because it permitted abortions in some circumstances. The *Borowski* case was not heard by the Supreme Court of Canada until after section 251 of the *Criminal Code* had been struck down in the *Morgentaler* case. The Court held in *Morgentaler* that the legislation affected women's right to security of the person and deprived them of that right in a manner inconsistent with the principles of fundamental justice. Therefore, when the *Borowski* case came to be heard, there was no longer any issue to be decided. The Court refused to embark upon an abstract analysis of the meaning of Charter rights in the absence of specific legislation or facts.

73. *Tremblay v. Daigle* (1989), 62 D.L.R. (4th) 634 (S.C.C.).

74. The issue affects not only women's right to choose abortion, and to resist men attempting to assert veto rights over abortion, but also women's ability to make decisions about their own health during pregnancy. For example, in *Re Baby R* (1988), 53 D.L.R. (4th) 69, 30 B.C.L.R. (2d) 237 (S.C.), the child protection authorities attempted to force a woman to undergo a Caesarian section by "apprehending" the fetus prior to birth. The British Columbia Supreme Court held that the legislation did not permit pre-birth apprehension. The case was referred to, seemingly with approval, by the Supreme Court of Canada in *Tremblay v. Daigle, ibid.*, at D.L.R. 663.

75. For example, the British Columbia Court of Appeal held that "liberty" includes the right to choose one's occupation and where to pursue it. Legislation which restricted medical billing numbers to existing doctors and a limited number of others was struck down. *Wilson v. Medical Services Commission of B.C.* (1989), 30 B.C.L.R. (2d) 1, 53 D.L.R. (4th) 171, [1989] 2 W.W.R. 1, leave to appeal to S.C.C. refused November 3, 1988.

76. For example, in the *Wilson* case, *ibid.* at B.C.L.R. 18, the British Columbia Court of Appeal said of section 7: "It does not, however, extend to protect property or pure economic rights."

Notes

77. *R. v. Morgentaler, supra*, note 56 at S.C.R. 166.

78. *Ibid.*, at 171.

79. *Ibid.*, at 172.

80. Two of the five justices in the majority (Dickson C.J.C. and Lamer J.) concluded that state interference with bodily integrity and serious state-imposed psychological stress, in the criminal law context, constitute a breach of security of the person. Section 251 violated a pregnant woman's rights to security of the person because she was prevented from undergoing a generally safe medical procedure that might be of clear benefit to her unless she met criteria entirely unrelated to her own priorities and aspirations. Also, the operation of the decision-making mechanism created dangerous delays. Another two of the majority (Beetz and Estey JJ.) thought that the procedural requirements of section 251 significantly delayed pregnant women's access to medical treatment, thus resulting in an additional danger to their health and depriving them of their right to security of the person. The *Morgentaler* case did not turn on the equality rights of section 15. The impact of using an equality rights analysis of the abortion issue could be considerable.

81. *Hunter v. Southam Inc.*, [1984] 2 S.C.R. 145.

82. For a discussion of the U.S. situation, see Frances Olsen, "Unravelling Compromise" (1989) *Harvard L. Rev.* 105.

83. Sections 9 and 12 read:

    9. Everyone has the right not to be arbitrarily detained or imprisoned.

    12. Everyone has the right not to be subjected to any cruel and unusual treatment or punishment.

84. Section 10 reads:

    Everyone has the right on arrest or detention

    (a) to be informed promptly of the reasons therefor;

    (b) to retain and instruct counsel without delay and to be informed of that right; and

    (c) to have the validity of the detention determined by way of habeas corpus and to be released if the detention is not lawful.

85. Because it applies to persons "charged with an offence", section 11 has been held to apply only to criminal proceedings or to proceedings where a conviction may lead to a true penal consequence. *R. v. Wigglesworth* (1987), 37 C.C.C. (3d) 385, 45 D.L.R. (4th) 235, [1987] 2 S.C.R. 541. Section 11 reads:

    11. Any person charged with an offence has the right

    (a) to be informed without unreasonable delay of the specific offence;

    (b) to be tried within a reasonable time;

    (c) not to be compelled to be a witness in proceedings against that person in respect of the offence;

(d) to be presumed innocent until proven guilty according to law in a fair and public hearing by an independent and impartial tribunal;

(e) not to be denied reasonable bail without just cause;

(f) except in the case of an offence under military law tried before a military tribunal, to the benefit of trial by jury where the maximum punishment for the offence is imprisonment for five years or a more severe punishment;

(g) not to be found guilty on account of any act or omission unless, at the time of the act or omission, it constituted an offence under Canadian or international law or was criminal according to the general principles of law recognized by the community of nations;

(h) if finally acquitted of the offence, not to be tried for it again, and, if found guilty and punished for the offence, not to be tried or punished for it again; and

(i) if found guilty of the offence and if the punishment for the offence has been varied between the time of commission and the time of sentencing, to the benefit of the lesser punishment.

86. When the survivor of sexual assault doesn't report the crime quickly, that has led to arguments that the accused's rights under section 11(b) were violated. However, the courts have held that the delay should be counted from the time the person is charged, rather than from when the offence occurred, so those arguments have failed: *R. v. Carter* [1986] 1 S.C.R. 981, 26 C.C.C. (3d) 572, [1986] 4 W.W.R. 673, 29 D.L.R. (4th) 309. In this case, there had been a delay of almost three years between the date of the offence and the charge. The Court rejected the accused's section 11(b) argument, but said that pre-charge delay might have an impact on the right to a fair hearing under section 11(d).

87. *R. v. Seaboyer*, [1991] 2 S.C.R. 577.

88. The compulsion to testify regardless of whether the answers may tend to incriminate is found in the *Canada Evidence Act* and in the comparable provincial statute.

89. Spouses can be compelled to testify in all civil cases (in most provinces) and in criminal cases where the charge relates to a crime of violence against the spouse, to child abuse, or to sexual assault in a number of cases: *Canada Evidence Act*, R.S.C. C.E-10, s. 4.

90. For example, see Catharine MacKinnon, "Excerpts from the Presentation to the Ontario Select Committee on Constitutional Reform", *Resources for Feminist Research*, vol. 17, no. 3 (Sept. 1988), p. 144:

> The Canadian Charter of Rights and Freedoms is advanced beyond any comparable instrument in the world today in promising women full citizenship. Its combination of equal protection of the law with specific nondiscrimination guarantees, together with its substantive recognition of disadvantage and support for affirmative relief, lays the legal foundation for some of the most significant advances in sex equality ever to be made for women under law.

91. Two important cases that are working their way through the courts are: *Symes v. Canada* [1989] 1 C.T.C. 476 (Fed. T.D.) (the right of a self-employed person to deduct the full amount of child-care expenses as a business expense), and *Doe v. Board of Commissioners of Police for Metropolitan Toronto et al.* (1989), 58 D.L.R. (4th) 396 (Ont. H.C.) (a claim that the police were negligent and caused damage to a woman who was assaulted in her apartment by a serial rapist who had assaulted other women in the vicinity).

92. Gwen Brodsky and Shelagh Day, *Canadian Charter Equality Rights for Women: One Step Forward or Two Steps Back?* (Ottawa: Canadian Advisory Council on the Status of Women, 1989). For a more recent review of the equality cases and comparisons with the U.S. approach, see L. Smith, "Adding a Third Dimension: The Canadian Approach to Constitutional Equality Guarantees" (1992), 55 *Law and Contemporary Problems* 211.

93. For fuller discussions of this point, see L. Smith, "Judicial Interpretation of Equality Rights under the Canadian Charter of Rights and Freedoms: Some Clear and Present Dangers" (1988) 23 *U.B.C.L. Rev.* 65, and W. Black and L. Smith, "The Equality Rights", in *The Canadian Charter of Rights and Freedoms*, ed. G.A. Beaudoin and E. Ratushny, 2nd ed. (Toronto: Carswell, 1989), p. 557.

94. *Andrews v. Law Society of B.C.* [1989] 1 S.C.R. 143, 2 W.W.R. 289, 56 D.L.R. (4th) 1, 34 B.C.L.R. (2d) 273; *R. v. Turpin*, [1989] 1 S.C.R. 1296, 69 C.R. (3d) 97, 48 C.C.C. (3d) 8; *Reference re Workers' Compensation Act, 1983 (Nfld.), ss. 32, 34* (1989), 56 D.L.R. (4th) 765.

95. Wilson J. in *Turpin, ibid.*, at S.C.R. 1332.

96. In *Andrews, supra,* note 94, the Supreme Court of Canada defined discrimination as follows (at S.C.R. 174-5):

   I would say then that discrimination may be described as a distinction, whether intentional or not but based on grounds relating to personal characteristics of the individual or group, which has the effect of imposing burdens, obligations, or disadvantages on such individual or group not imposed upon others, or which withholds or limits access to opportunities, benefits, and advantages available to other members of society. Distinctions based on personal characteristics attributed to an individual solely on the basis of association with a group will rarely escape the charge of discrimination, while those based on an individual's merits and capacities will rarely be so classed.

97. *Brooks v. Canada Safeway Ltd.*, [1989] 4 W. W. R. 193, 59 D. L. R. (4th) 321, 1 S.C.R. 1219.

98. *Janzen v. Platy Enterprises Ltd.*, [1989] 4 W.W.R. 39 at 64-65.

99. *Constitution Act, 1982*, section 43 (b).

100. The circumstances are: (1) the parent's first language is that of the linguistic minority (English or French), or the parent received primary school instruction in Canada and the language in which they received that instruction is the language of the linguistic minority of the province where they now reside; and (2) the number of children to whom the minority language educational rights applies warrants the provision of public funds for minority language instruction. Part of section 23 (relating to situations where the parent's first language is that of the linguistic minority) is not yet in effect in Quebec. The Supreme Court of Canada, in one of its first decisions under the Charter, struck down Quebec legislation that attempted to redefine the classes of persons entitled to have their children instructed in English. *Attorney General of Quebec v. Quebec Association of Protestant School Boards et al.* (1984), 10 D.L.R. (4th) 321.

However, there have been mixed results for linguistic minorities outside Quebec who have attempted to use section 23 to obtain French-language instruction for their children (as opposed to access to French immersion programs), with separate school boards to control and manage French-language education: see *Mahe v. Alta.*, [1990] 3 W.W.R. 97, 1 S.C.R. 342.

101. *Lavell v. A.G. Canada*, [1974] S.C.R. 1349, 38 D.L.R. (3d) 481.

102. *Lovelace v. Canada*, [1983] *Can. Hum. Rts. Y.B.* 305.

103. *An Act to Amend the Indian Act*, S.C. 1985, c. 27.

104. *Reference re Bill 30, An Act to Amend the Education Act (Ont.)* [1987] 1 S.C.R. 1148.

105. As was argued in *R. v. Keegstra, supra*, note 63.

106. See *Edwards Books & Art Ltd. v. The Queen, supra*, note 53.

107. *Hunter v. Southam Inc., supra*, note 81.

108. *Black v. The Law Society of Alberta* [1989] 4 W.W.R. 1.

109. Section 32 of the Charter, as interpreted by the Supreme Court of Canada in *R.W.D.S.U., Local 580 v. Dolphin Delivery Ltd.*, [1986] 2 S.C.R. 573.

110. Although human rights legislation itself must comply with the Charter. See *Re Blainey and Ont. Hockey Assn.* (1986), 26 D.L.R. (4th) 728 (Ont. C.A.), leave to appeal to S.C.C. refused (1986), 58 O.R. (2d) 274 (headnote).

How the Canadian Constitution Got This Way

1. Jan Noel, "New France: Les Femmes Favorisées", in *Rethinking Canada: The Promise of Women's History*, ed. Veronica Strong-Boag and Anita Clair Fellman (Toronto: Copp Clark Pitman, 1986), pp. 23-44.

2. Alison Prentice et al., *Canadian Women: A History* (Toronto: Harcourt Brace Javanovich, 1988), pp. 65-84.

3. It appears that both Black people and First Nations people were held as slaves in what became Upper and Lower Canada. Some Black people came as free settlers, others as slaves. Aboriginal slaves were called "panis", a derivative of "Pawnees", as most were of that nation. In 1793, the legislature of Upper Canada became the first in the British Empire to limit slavery. The bill was a compromise between the interests of principle and the interests of private property. It provided for gradual abolition, requiring that slaves who entered Upper Canada be freed upon entry, that children of slaves be freed at the age of 25, and that their children be freed at birth. By the time slavery was abolished in the British Empire in 1843 it was no longer practised in Canada, and now is a little-known but shameful chapter of Canadian history. See Robin W. Winks, *The Blacks in Canada* (Montreal: McGill-Queen's University Press, 1971), pp. 2-16, and James Walker, *A History of Blacks in Canada* (Hull: Minister of State Multiculturalism, 1980).

4. Peter W. Hogg, *Constitutional Law of Canada*, 2nd ed. (Toronto: Carswell, 1985), pp. 21-22.

Notes

5. Douglas Sanders, "Indian Women: A Brief History of Their Roles and Rights", (1975) 21 *McGill Law Journal* 659.

6. Hogg, *supra*, note 4, p. 190.

7. Gordon T. Stewart, *The Origins of Canadian Politics: A Comparative Approach* (Vancouver: University of British Columbia Press, 1986), p. 3.

8. *The Clergy Endowments (Canada) Act*, 1791, 31 Geo. III, c. 83 (U.K.).

9. Prentice et al., *supra*, note 2, p. 98.

10. *Ibid.*, pp. 98-99.

11. *Ibid.*, p. 99.

12. *An Act to repeal certain Acts therein mentioned, and to amend, consolidate, and reduce into one Act, the several Statutory provisions now in force for the regulation of Elections of Members to represent the People of this Province in the Legislative Assembly thereof*, (1849) 12 Vict., c. 27, s. 46 (Prov. of Canada). This act specifically excluded women from voting in any county, riding, city, or town.

13. Prentice et al., *supra*, note 2, pp. 98-101.

14. *Ibid.*

15. Sylvia Van Kirk, "The Role of Native Women in the Fur Trade Society of Western Canada, 1670-1830", in *Rethinking Canada*, *supra*, note 1, pp. 59-66.

16. Prentice et al., *supra*, note 2, pp. 98-101.

17. *Ibid.*, p. 174.

18. Kenneth McNaught, *The Pelican History of Canada* (Baltimore: Penguin Books, 1969), p. 131.

19. Quoted in *Hillsdale College v. Department of Health, etc.* 696 F. (2d) 418 (1982) at 431.

20. Arthur R.M. Lower, *Colony to Nation: A History of Canada*, 5th ed. (Toronto: McClelland and Stewart, 1977).

21. Prentice et al., *supra*, note 2, p. 175.

22. In *Re Mabel P. French* (1905), 37 N.B.R. 359 at 365-366, quoting Mr. Justice Bradley, *Bradwell v. State of Illinois* 16 Wall. 130.

23. Sylvia B. Bashevkin, *Toeing the Lines: Women and Party Politics in English Canada* (Toronto: University of Toronto Press, 1985), p. 11.

24. *Dominion Elections Act*, R.S.C. 1906, c. 6 amended by 10-11 Geo. V., c. 46.

25. Canada, Royal Commission on the Status of Women, *Report of the Royal Commission on the Status of Women in Canada* (Ottawa: 1970), p. 337.

26. J. Patrick Boyer, *Election Law in Canada: The Law and Procedure of Federal, Provincial and Territorial Elections* (Toronto: Butterworths, 1987), vol. 1, p. 387.

27. Canada, Royal Commission on the Status of Women in Canada, *supra*, note 25, p. 337.

28. Bashevkin, *supra*, note 23, pp. 8-10.

29. Prentice et al., *supra*, note 2, p. 280.

30. Penney Kome, *Women of Influence: Canadian Women and Politics* (Toronto: Doubleday, 1985), p. 198.

31. *Ibid.*, pp. 76-80.

32. Canada, Royal Commission on the Status of Women in Canada, *supra*, note 25, p. vii.

33. *Ibid.*, p. 355.

34. *Ibid.*, p. 356.

35. Hogg, *supra*, note 4, p. 639. The Co-operative Commonwealth Federation (CCF) first espoused a Bill of Rights in 1945: Roger E. Salhany, *The Origin of Rights* (Toronto: Carswell, 1986), p. 7.

36. S.C. 1960, c. 44, s. 1(b).

37. Until 1984, in fact, the Supreme Court of Canada found a federal law to be inconsistent with the *Canadian Bill of Rights* on only **one** occasion: *R. v. Drybones*, [1970] S.C.R. 282. This case was virtually interpreted out of existence in subsequent decisions.

38. It is illustrative that such a notable civil libertarian and progressive individual as Thomas Berger published a book about Canadian "minorities and dissenters, ... their struggles, their victories, their defeats", in which the struggles of women for equality were never mentioned: Thomas R. Berger, *Fragile Freedoms: Human Rights and Dissent in Canada* (Toronto: Clarke, Irwin & Co., 1981), p. xvi.

39. In the first, Jeanette Lavell, an Aboriginal woman, challenged a provision of the *Indian Act* that deprived Indian women who married non-Indian men of their Indian status, although an Indian man who married a non-Indian woman not only kept his status but conferred it on his wife and children. The Supreme Court of Canada held that the provision did not contravene the *Canadian Bill of Rights*, because all Indian women were treated the same way and the equality guarantee extended only to equality in the **administration** of the law, not to the law's **content**. The second case, *Bliss v. A.G. Canada*, involved a woman who had worked long enough to claim ordinary unemployment insurance benefits, but not long enough to claim the special maternity benefits. When Stella Bliss applied for the ordinary benefits shortly after the birth of her child she was turned down despite the fact she had paid the premiums and was available for and capable of employment, according to her doctor. A section of the *Unemployment Insurance Act* said that pregnant and recently-delivered women could not receive the ordinary benefits. Arguing that she was discriminated against because she was pregnant, and that this constituted sex discrimination, Ms. Bliss ultimately took her case to the Supreme Court of Canada. That Court held that discrimination against pregnant women was not sex discrimination, saying that "Any inequality between the sexes in this area is not created by legislation but by nature", effectively sealing off many facets of women's lives from protection under the *Canadian Bill of Rights*. (The *Bliss* decision [(1978) 92 D.L.R. (3d) 417 (SCC)] has now been overruled in *Brooks v. Canada Safeway Limited*.)

Notes

40. *Murdoch v. Murdoch*, [1974] 1 S.C.R. 423, 41 D.L.R. (3d) 367.

41. Canada, Parliament, Special Joint Committee of the Senate and of the House of Commons on the Constitution of Canada, *The Special Joint Committee of the Senate and of the House of Commons on the Constitution of Canada: Final Report* (Ottawa: 1972), p. 20.

42. Canadian Bar Association, Committee on the Constitution, Towards a New Canada (Montreal: 1978).

43. It concluded that the inclusion of a "provision providing for equality before the law" would be desirable, going on to say: "The phrase, it is true, is somewhat vague. The law can never fully treat people equally, and must differentiate for a variety of reasons. But the courts would as in other cases accept reasonable limitations." *Ibid.*, p. 20.

44. Canada, Statistics Canada, *Women in Canada: A Statistical Report*, 2nd ed. (Ottawa: 1990), p. 78.

45. *Ibid.*, p. 97.

46. Bashevkin, *supra*, note 23, pp. 58, 60, and 73.

47. For accounts of the history of the formation of the new constitution, see Keith Banting and Richard Simeon, eds., *And No One Cheered: Federalism, Democracy and the Constitutional Act* (Toronto: Methuen, 1983), particularly Chaviva Hosek, "Women and the Constitutional Process", pp. 280-300; Roy Romanow, John Whyte, and Howard Leeson, Canada... *Notwithstanding: The Making of the Constitution 1976-1982* (Toronto: Carswell/Methuen, 1984); Robert Sheppard and Michael Valpy, *The National Deal: The Fight for a Canadian Constitution* (Toronto: Fleet Books, 1982).

48. *Reference re Amendment of the Constitution of Canada (Nos. 1, 2, 3) Patriation Reference Case* (1981), 125 D.L.R. (3d) 1, (1981) 1 S.C.R. 753, (1981) 6 W.W.R. 1 at D.L.R. 84.

49. Roger Tassé, "Application of the Canadian Charter of Rights and Freedoms", in *The Canadian Charter of Rights and Freedoms*, ed. G.A. Beaudoin and E. Ratushny, 2nd ed. (Toronto: Carswell, 1989), p. 102.

50. Penney Kome, *The Taking of Twenty-Eight: Women Challenge the Constitution* (Toronto: Women's Press, 1983).

51. Susan Delacourt and Graham Fraser, "Marathon talks were all part of plan, PM says", *The Globe and Mail*, June 12, 1990, pp. A1 and A8.

52. For example, in *The Vision and the Game: Making the Canadian Constitution* (Calgary: Detselig Enterprises, 1987), the authors (Lenard Cohen, Patrick Smith and Paul Warwick) interview "the framers of the accord reached in November, 1981", described as "elected political leaders, senior public servants, interest group representatives and constitutional specialists". The list of participants includes 29 persons, two of whom are women. They are Mary Eberts, described as "Women's Rights Lawyer" and Tamara Thompson, described as "Women's Rights Leader". None of the politicians, advisers, public servants, or academics listed is female.

53. A characterization that: (a) implicitly but falsely lumps women with true lobbyists in pursuit of special interests such as the Canadian Manufacturers' Association or the Canadian Medical

Association; (b) ignores the fact that women form a majority of the population; (c) accepts the predefined terms of the debate, whereby regional interests are legitimately at the table, but the interests of people defined in other ways (e.g., by sex or Aboriginal status) are not.

54. Mary Eberts, "Excerpts from the Presentation to the Ontario Select Committee on Constitutional Reform", *Resources for Feminist Research* (Sept. 1988), vol. 17, no. 3, p. 145.

Conclusion

1. Alan C. Cairns, "Citizens (Outsiders) and Governments (Insiders) in Constitution-Making: The Case of Meech Lake", *Canadian Public Policy* (Sept. 1988), vol. XIV, p. S121. See also Alan C. Cairns, "The Limited Constitutional Vision of Meech Lake", in *Competing Constitutional Visions: The Meech Lake Accord,* ed. Katherine E. Swinton and Carol J. Rogerson (Toronto: Carswell, 1988).

2. Iris Marion Young, "Polity and group difference: A Critique of the Ideal of Universal Citizenship", in *Feminism and Political Theory*, ed. Cass R. Sunstein (Chicago: University of Chicago Press, 1990), p. 124.

3. Beverley Baines, "After Meech Lake: The Ms/Representation of Gender in Scholarly Spaces", in *After Meech Lake: Lessons for the Future*, ed. David E. Smith et al. (Saskatoon: Fifth House Publishers, 1991), pp. 205-218.

4. See, for example, Jill McCalla Vickers, "Feminist Approaches to Women in Politics", in *Beyond the Vote: Canadian Women and Politics*, ed. Linda Kealey and Joan Sangster (Toronto: University of Toronto Press, 1989), p. 16.

5. *Ibid.*, p. 31.

6. Canadian Advisory Council on the Status of Women, *Brief to the Royal Commission on Electoral Reform and Party Financing* (Ottawa: 1990).

7. For a detailed study of women's participation in politics in Canada and other parts of the world, of the barriers encountered and some possible ways of removing them, see Chantal Maillé and Valentina Pollon, *Primed for Power: Women in Canadian Politics* (Ottawa: Canadian Advisory Council on the Status of Women, 1990).

8. Christine Boyle, "Home Rule for Women: Power-Sharing Between Men and Women" (1983) 7 *Dalhousie L.J.* 790.

9. *Ibid.*, p. 796.

10. See *Constitution Act, 1867* s. 91(24) *Charter* s. 25 and *Constitution Act, 1982*, s. 35.

11. See *Constitution Act, 1867* s. 133 and *Charter* ss. 16-21, 23.

12. See *Constitution Act, 1867* s. 93.

13. *Andrews v. Law Society of B.C.* [1989] 1 S. C. R. 143, 2 W. W. R. 289, 56 D.L.R. (4th) 1, 34 B. C. L. R. (2d) 273.

Bibliography

Baines, Beverley. "After Meech Lake: The Ms/Representation of Gender in Scholarly Spaces". In *After Meech Lake: Lessons for the Future*. Ed. David E. Smith et al. Saskatoon: Fifth House Publishers, 1991.

Banting, Keith and Richard Simeon, eds. *And No One Cheered: Federalism, Democracy and the Constitutional Act*. Toronto: Methuen, 1983.

Bashevkin, Sylvia B. *Toeing the Lines: Women and Party Politics in English Canada*. Toronto: University of Toronto Press, 1985.

Berger, Thomas R. *Fragile Freedoms: Human Rights and Dissent in Canada*. Toronto: Clarke, Irwin & Co., 1981.

Black, W. and L. Smith. "The Equality Rights". In *The Canadian Charter of Rights and Freedoms*. Ed. G.A. Beaudoin and E. Ratushny. 2nd ed. Toronto: Carswell, 1989.

Boyer, J. Patrick. *Election Law in Canada: The Law and Procedure of Federal, Provincial and Territorial Elections*. Toronto: Butterworths, 1987.

Boyle, Christine. "Home Rule for Women: Power-Sharing Between Men and Women" (1983) 7 *Dalhousie L.J.* 790.

Brodsky, Gwen and Shelagh Day. *Canadian Charter Equality Rights for Women: One Step Forward or Two Steps Back?* Ottawa: Canadian Advisory Council on the Status of Women, 1989.

Cairns, Alan C. "Citizens (Outsiders) and Governments (Insiders) in Constitution-Making: The Case of Meech Lake". *Canadian Public Policy*, vol. XIV, Sept. 1988.

Cairns, Alan C. "The Limited Constitutional Vision of Meech Lake". In *Competing Constitutional Visions: The Meech Lake Accord*. Ed. Katherine E. Swinton and Carol J. Rogerson. Toronto: Carswell, 1988.

Cairns, Alan C. and Douglas Williams, eds. *Constitution, Government, and Society in Canada: Selected Essays*. Toronto: McClelland and Stewart, 1988.

Canada. Parliament. Special Joint Committee of the Senate and of the House of Commons on the Constitution of Canada. *The Special Joint Committee of the Senate and of the House of Commons on the Constitution of Canada: Final Report*. Ottawa: 1972.

Canada. Royal Commission on the Status of Women in Canada. *Report of the Royal Commission on the Status of Women in Canada*. Ottawa: 1970.

Canada. Statistics Canada. *Women in Canada: A Statistical Report*. 2nd ed. Ottawa: 1990.

Canada. Task Force on Barriers to Women in the Public Service. *Beneath the Veneer: The Report of the Task Force on Barriers to Women in the Public Service*. Ottawa: 1990.

Canadian Advisory Council on the Status of Women. *Brief to the Royal Commission on Electoral Reform and Party Financing*. Ottawa: 1990.

Canadian Bar Association. Committee on the Constitution. *Towards a New Canada*. Montreal: Canadian Bar Foundation, 1978.

Cohen, Lenard; Patrick Smith; and Paul Warwick. *The Vision and the Game: Making the Canadian Constitution*. Calgary: Detselig Enterprises, 1987.

Corry, J.A. "The Uses of a Constitution". *Special Lectures of the Law Society of Upper Canada 1978*. Toronto: Richard DeBoo, 1978.

Delacourt, Susan and Graham Fraser. "Marathon Talks Were All Part of Plan, PM Says". *The Globe and Mail*, June 12, 1990.

Eberts, Mary. "Excerpts from the Presentation to the Ontario Select Committee on Constitutional Reform", *Resources for Feminist Research*, vol. 17, no. 3, Sept. 1988, pp. 145-146.

Forsey, Eugene A. "The Courts and the Conventions of the Constitution" (1984), 33 *U.N.B.L.J.* 11 at 41.

Greschner, Donna. "A Walk Through the Charter". In *Charter of Rights: Who Cares? A Post-Conference Recap*. Regina Business and Professional Women's Club. Regina: 1985.

Hogg, Peter W. *Constitutional Law of Canada*. 2nd ed. Toronto: Carswell, 1985.

Kome, Penney. *The Taking of Twenty-Eight: Women Challenge the Constitution*. Toronto: Women's Press, 1983.

Kome, Penney. *Women of Influence: Canadian Women and Politics*. Toronto: Doubleday, 1985.

Lower, Arthur R.M. *Colony to Nation: A History of Canada*. 5th ed. Toronto: McClelland and Stewart, 1977.

MacKinnon, Catharine. "Excerpts from the Presentation to the Ontario Select Committee on Constitutional Reform". *Resources for Feminist Research*, vol. 17, no. 3, Sept. 1988.

Maillé, Chantal and Valentina Pollon. *Primed for Power: Women in Canadian Politics*. Ottawa: Canadian Advisory Council on the Status of Women, 1990.

McCalla Vickers, Jill. "Feminist Approaches to Women in Politics". In *Beyond the Vote: Canadian Women and Politics*. Ed. Linda Kealey and Joan Sangster. Toronto: University of Toronto Press, 1989.

McNaught, Kenneth. *The Pelican History of Canada*. Baltimore: Penguin Books, 1969.

Noel, Jan. "New France: Les Femmes Favorisées". In *Rethinking Canada: The Promise of Women's History*. Ed. Veronica Strong-Boag and Anita Clair Fellman. Toronto: Copp Clark Pitman, 1986.

Olsen, Frances. "Unravelling Compromise" (1989) *Harvard L. Rev.* 105.

Prentice, Alison et al. *Canadian Women: A History*. Toronto: Harcourt Brace Javanovich, 1988.

"Report and Record of the Committee of Investigation into the Conduct of the Hon. Mr. Justice Berger and Resolution of the Canadian Judicial Council" (1983) 28 *McGill Law Journal* 378.

Roberts, Barbara. *Smooth Sailing or Storm Warning? Canadian and Quebec Women's Groups on the Meech Lake Accord*. Ottawa: Canadian Research Institute for the Advancement of Women, 1989.

Romanow, Roy; John Whyte; and Howard Leeson. *Canada... Notwithstanding: The Making of the Constitution 1976-1982*. Toronto: Carswell/Methuen, 1984.

Russell, Peter H. and Jacob S. Ziegel. "Federal Judicial Appointments: An Appraisal of the First Mulroney Government's Appointments". Draft Paper for the Canadian Association of Law Teachers, May 1989.

Salhany, Roger E. *The Origin of Rights*. Toronto: Carswell, 1986.

Sanders, Douglas. "Indian Women: A Brief History of Their Roles and Rights". (1975) 21 *McGill Law Journal* 659.

Sheppard, Robert and Michael Valpy. *The National Deal: The Fight for a Canadian Constitution*. Toronto: Fleet Books, 1982.

Smith, L. "Judicial Interpretation of Equality Rights under the Canadian Charter of Rights and Freedoms: Some Clear and Present Dangers" (1988) 23 *U.B.C.L. Rev.* 65.

Smith, L. "The Distinct Society Clause in the Meech Lake Accord: Could It Affect Equality Rights for Women?". In *Competing Constitutional Visions: The Meech Lake Accord*. Ed. K.E. Swinton and C.J. Rogerson. Toronto: Carswell, 1988.

Stewart, Gordon T. *The Origins of Canadian Politics: A Comparative Approach*. Vancouver: University of British Columbia Press, 1986.

Sturgess, Garry and Philip Chubb, eds. *Judging the World: Law and Politics in the World's Leading Courts*. Toronto: Butterworths, 1988.

Tassé, Roger. "Application of the Canadian Charter of Rights and Freedoms". In *The Canadian Charter of Rights and Freedoms*. Ed. G.A. Beaudoin and E. Ratushny. 2nd ed. Toronto: Carswell, 1989.

Van Kirk, Sylvia. "The Role of Native Women in the Fur Trade Society of Western Canada, 1670-1830". In *Rethinking Canada: The Promise of Women's History*. Ed. Veronica Strong-Boag and Anita Clair Fellman. Toronto: Copp Clark Pitman, 1986.

Walker, James. *A History of Blacks in Canada*. Hull: Minister of State Multiculturalism, 1980.

Watts, Ronald L. "The American Constitution in Comparative Perspective: A Comparison of Federalism in the United States and Canada". *Journal of American History*, vol. 74, 1987.

Wheare, K.C. *Modern Constitutions*. London: Oxford University Press, 1966.

Wilson, Madam Justice Bertha. "Will Women Judges Really Make a Difference?". The Fourth Annual Barbara Betcherman Memorial Lecture, Osgoode Hall Law School, February 8, 1990.

Winks, Robin W. *The Blacks in Canada*. Montreal: McGill-Queen's University Press, 1971.

Woodcock, George. *The Century That Made Us: Canada 1814-1914*. Don Mills, Ont.: Oxford University Press, 1989.

Woodward, Jack. *Native Law*. Toronto: Carswell, 1989.

Young, Iris Marion. "Polity and Group Difference: A Critique of the Ideal of Universal Citizenship". In *Feminism and Political Theory*. Ed. Cass R. Sunstein. Chicago: University of Chicago Press, 1990.

Bibliotheque Municipale de Field